T0148227

## Other books by Ian Oldham

Shifting Gears—
High Performance skills for the 21st century:
Bateman Publishing

For information on our
Shifting Gears programmes go to
www.shiftinggears.co.nz

# 5 tools to change your world

## Taking control of what you experience

### Ian Oldham

Order this book online at www.trafford.com
or email orders@trafford.com

Most Trafford titles are also available at major online book retailers.

© Copyright 2012 Ian Oldham.
All rights reserved. No part of this publication may be reproduced, stored in a
retrieval system, or transmitted, in any form or by any means, electronic, mechanical,
photocopying, recording, or otherwise, without the written prior permission of the author.

This book is designed to provide information for the use of the reader
and is the sole expression and opinion of the author. It is sold with the
understanding that neither the publisher nor the author is engaged to render
any type of psychological or other professional advice and they are not
liable for any physical, financial, psychological, emotional or commercial
damages, including, but not limited to, special, incidental, consequential or
other damages. You are responsible for your choices, actions, and results.

Cover design and illustrations: Heather Thomson

Printed in the United States of America.

ISBN: 978-1-4669-7067-0 (sc)
ISBN: 978-1-4669-7194-3 (e)

*Trafford rev. 01/23/2013*

 www.trafford.com

**North America & international**
toll-free: 1 888 232 4444 (USA & Canada)
phone: 250 383 6864 ♦ fax: 812 355 4082

# Acknowledgements

This book came about with the support of a special group of people: a group headed up by my wife Valma who offered support at the appropriate moments and once again put up with me as I dropped into the rather anti-social state required to focus on writing.

Other members of the group were Barbara Gordon, Gill Garchow, Glenys Gwynne, Graham Parkins, Lori Howells, Murray Presland, Regan Hughes and Susannah Engel. Besides being trusted friends, what they have in common is an attribute that I greatly value: their willingness to give clear, unambiguous feedback without feeling any need to sugarcoat it. Knowing this gave me the confidence that I was on the right track and that the finished product would be worthwhile.

As editor, Louisa Gaimster, of Red Pen Proofreading and Editing Services, has been a key person in the process and it has been a delight to work with her. The close collaboration between writer and editor involves a delicate balance on the part of both parties and Louisa was superb. She managed to keep me grammatically in line and offer the occasional suggestion without altering the essence of what I was trying to say.

A special thank you to Heather Thomson; her work on the cover and on the diagrams neatly grasped the essence of what I wanted to illustrate and brought the concepts to life.

Over the years, I have worked with many people and shared many conversations over cups of coffee. To all those people, thank you. Your stories and insights are the stuff of this book.

And, last but not least, as the reader, you are the final arbiter of whether or not this book has been of benefit. With that in mind, I would greatly appreciate your feedback; observations, stories, what didn't work, what did work and suggestions for improvements.

Best wishes
Ian

# Contents

# Introduction and overview

The cover picture is of Shivling, a mountain set high above the Gangotri glacier in Northern India in an area of overwhelming beauty and grandeur. The scene captures the disparate notions of being 'out there' doing something practical while taking the time to reflect on things and place them in perspective. It is very easy to focus on the tools in the book as an end in themselves and lose sight of their purpose which is to add value to your life by making it more enjoyable and productive. Otherwise, why bother?

## Firmly in the driver's seat

This book is not about 'fixing' you or anyone else. It is about keeping you firmly in the driver's seat as you add to, or evolve, your kit of tools for dealing with the everyday difficulties that are a part of the human condition. Focusing on the destination as well as the journey, the book is pragmatic and dross free, with concepts and skills that are simple, powerful and instantly applied.

## Taking control of what we experience

So often people think or assume that what they experience is a matter of fate, something to be endured: something over which they have no control. This idea can lead to a state of 'learned helplessness' typified by sayings along the lines of "What's the point? It never works!" or "They don't care!" or even "They made me angry!" (an expression of perceived loss of control over how they feel). This book shows that what you experience is connected to you and that you can control it. This concept alone often comes as a profound insight, if not a shock, to many people, if not intellectually then emotionally.

## Fully functioning adults

Treating yourself and others as fully functioning adults is a recurring theme as we explore the tools (concepts and skills) that enable you to take control of what you experience. By fully functioning adult I mean someone who takes responsibility for how they respond to what is happening to them rather than seeing themselves as a victim.

Many people tell me about how they have used the tools to improve specific aspects of their lives by taking the knowledge on board, adapting it and then applying what they have learnt to situations they needed to deal with. When I talk about learning, I am referring to the change of behaviour arising from the application of knowledge. This explains how the same knowledge can result in an infinite number of behavioural changes. The range of creative changes made by different people, all using the same tools, underscores this difference.

*If you know it but do not do it then you*
*have not learnt it*

To the question "What will you learn from this book?" perhaps the correct answer is "I have no idea—it depends!" No one else can tread your path for you in life or ever have a full understanding of what it is that you are dealing with or want to sort out; and that is the power of being treated as a fully functioning adult. Sure, there are times when each of us behaves as anything but a fully functioning adult, but it is still great to be treated as one.

## Uncertainty and surprise

Learning is uncertain and full of surprises, which is why I do not attempt to tell you how to live your life or tell you what you should do. 'Should' revolves around someone else's expectations, not yours. However, dip into the book, stimulate your thinking, have a bit of fun, reflect, and consider other viewpoints. Then, as you see fit, creatively change how you operate. Otherwise, to a large extent, I leave you to connect the dots.

## Looking to the future

Rather than looking to the past ("Why did this happen to me?") and indulging in lots of introspection, I deliberately focus on the future. You are where you are and that is that. However, from this point on, you are responsible for your life, for finding meaning to it, and for finding a way of navigating through it. No one else can do this for you and, if they could, they would be in control and you would be a victim.

The use of the word tools to describe the various skills and concepts covered is quite deliberate. With any tool it is entirely up to you as to what you do with it. So I explain the purpose of each tool, how it can be used and what to watch out for. However, it would be quite pointless telling you if a particular tool is important or not, what to use it on, or even when to use it. The tools are for your journey as you take control of what you experience.

Best wishes and be open
to the unexpected.
Ian

# A tale of two managers

Late one day two senior managers, having travelled in separate cars from the same nearby location, turned up at my office. They were there because, over a long period of time, their working relationship had deteriorated to the point at which they could no longer work together and they had not spoken to one another for several months. Their working colleagues had largely split into two camps, each supporting one of the 'combatants' and the situation was having a strongly negative impact on the company operation.

In sheer desperation, and after many months of meetings at which he had tried to facilitate an amicable settlement, one of the company directors called me and asked if I could help. Quite frankly, having heard his story, the situation sounded so serious and so locked up that it seemed hopeless. But for some reason about which I was unclear, I agreed that if the managers were willing I would at least give them an initial hearing. After all, something unexpected might happen.

Well, here they were in my office, each sitting at either end of the couch facing away from one another and pointedly avoiding eye contact. Things did not look promising and, in the face of this seemingly implacable wall, I momentarily felt at a loss as to what to do. However, I overcame this brief temptation to panic by remembering to trust the process, let go of any notion of an overall plan, and settle for taking things one step at a time. Thinking about the big picture and how to resolve it was just too hard and that was where the power of the tools—those concepts and skills covered in this book—came into their own.

To find out what happened, go straight to So, what happened? (p120). But before you do, you may care to flick through the book and then, in the light of whatever insights your reading and reflection generates, consider how you would have dealt with the situation. This way I am confident that you will gain far more from the book.

# Tool 1

# Step out of your Self-fulfilling Cycle

Of all the tools we cover, the Self-fulfilling Cycle lies at the heart of things on both the large scale of life's overall course and the small scale of immediate situations. The connections and opportunities for learning go on indefinitely.

## The Self-fulfilling Cycle

Situation ('As it is')

Next moment (situation) is created

Beliefs filter situation

*First opportunity - change the recording ...........*

Actions are selected

Feelings are triggered

*Second opportunity - seize the moment ...............*

Choices are narrowed

Thinking/ rationalising reinforces prejudices & views (self talk)

Feelings harden and create 'experience'

The Cycle makes sense of what happens and how we operate and its starting point is the current situation, 'As it is.' We use 'As it is' because it sounds neutral whereas, if we use the word reality, it comes loaded with philosophical baggage and can be the cause of much debate.

## As it is

When working with a group, to illustrate 'As it is,' I pick up a chair and place it squarely in front of one member of the group. Each person in the group will observe the event through their own set of filters. For instance, the person I place the chair in front of may think "Uh-oh! What's going to happen now?" or even "Why me?" Meanwhile others in the group may be thinking "Phew! Glad I'm not the focus of this," and so on with each person viewing and experiencing the event differently. However, apart from my moving the chair back to where it was, nothing else happens.

The moving of the chair was 'As it is'; all the other stuff, the various experiences, were created by the participants in their respective heads.

## A small scale example of the Self-fulfilling Cycle in operation

*At work, a person comes in looking a bit grumpy. You have never seen the person before but their appearance reminds you of a particularly aggressive person you used to know which immediately triggers the negative filters that you hold about that person. (Other words for these filters about how the world 'should' operate are beliefs, models or viewpoints. Acting like little prisms, filters distort your view of the world preventing you from seeing it 'As it is'.)*

*The person then says something that could be construed in several ways but, because your negative filters are operating, you interpret what is said as angry and treat the words as an attack. Exactly what you expected! Of course the person in question has no knowledge of all this because it is taking place in the privacy of your own mind.*

*Seeing the person as aggressive, you categorise whatever they say next as aggressive and set off around your Self-fulfilling Cycle. Instantly feeling angry, and with no thinking involved to this point, you reinforce, validate and generally firm up your feelings through self-talk (that little voice in your* head currently giving a running commentary on what you are reading right now). For example, you might think "How dare they talk to me like that! I have every right to be angry; in fact, anyone spoken to like that would get angry," along with many other thoughts in a similar vein, each justifying, adding to and hardening your viewpoint.

By now, your range of action choices is feeling quite limited because it really does seem that the only available feeling is angry. This drastically narrows your view of choices about what you do next. Acting peacefully while still angry is very difficult to do. Just think back to a time when you were angry. Now imagine acting peacefully instead. You will realise that now you are acting peacefully, you are feeling peaceful: angry feelings and peaceful actions are mutually exclusive. Of course, to the casual observer it is obvious that when it comes to how you could feel, you always have a limitless range of choices available—apoplectic rage, angry, a tad frustrated, calm, peaceful, loving, compassionate, and so on. But right now, you feel angry and that is how it is.

Here you are, feeling justifiably angry. You have thought the situation through (over a time ranging from milliseconds to days) and are now considering *what to do next. Well, the obvious action is to stand up for yourself—"Don't you talk to me like that!" At which point you are creating the next moment.*

*Meanwhile, the other person has also been following a Self-fulfilling Cycle, one set up earlier in the day with a background of stubbed toe when getting out of bed, argument with significant other at breakfast, backing over cat in driveway and now this.*

*What if, instead of playing out your part as described in the above scene, you responded differently?*

*The person comes into the room and behaves grumpily. Choosing to not buy into how they (apparently) feel, you override your initial reactions and decide that you will retain your equanimity and respond accordingly: after all, your day has been going along rather nicely up until then. With that mindset, you might respond with something like "You're sounding fed up. What's happened?" Said in a neutral way, this will create a different (and likely better) next moment. "Oh! It's been a rotten morning. Sorry if I sound a bit grumpy."*

When it comes to timing and reactions, nothing is certain in this world but the second scenario has a far better chance of enhancing a situation than the first. Trouble is it can all happen so fast—round the Cycle in a fraction of a second—followed by a suitable amount of time for regrets by all concerned.

## Becoming self-aware

Creating changes in how you operate requires self-awareness. This involves moving outside your Self-fulfilling Cycle to see what is happening and acknowledging how you are feeling at that moment. Not what you *think* about what is happening, rather you being aware of your emotional state. Combined, these two steps make you self-aware and place you in a position from which you can choose another way forward.

A prerequisite to reflecting upon the current situation, self-awareness enables us to make changes to how we operate. Without it we are stuck in the present. Be careful to not confuse reflection, which is highly constructive and purposeful, with rumination, which is simply a waste of your time and energy. Think back on those 'four o'clock in the morning' low points rehashing events to no useful purpose.

Self-awareness is what sets us apart from animals—and yes I have had a few interesting discussions on this point—but I will move right along anyway. We used to have a cat called 'Tigger.' He was somewhat set in his ways and I never noticed him reflecting on his day. Each morning he would stick his head out of the doorway, sniff the air and set off for another fight with next door's cat. Never saw him having a chat about territorial boundaries, or how they could work together. Some people seem to operate like that. "This is how I am, sunshine, so you may as well get used to it." I have even heard people who, having just completed a personality profile, use the results to justify their obnoxious behaviour.

Unhelpfully, the opposite to the above can also happen inasmuch as when you change your behaviour, some of those around you will try to keep you in the same old pigeonhole; otherwise they would have to revise their viewpoint and that can be so annoying for them.

## Opportunities for change

Once you are aware, there are two opportunities to break the Self-fulfilling Cycle, to act differently, and in ways aligned with your considered, more helpful style—the one that your rational self would like to follow. One opportunity, changing the recording, is longer term while the other is immediate and involves seizing the moment to alter your self-talk.

## First opportunity—change the recording

The first opportunity is to change your recording: those filters (beliefs/models/viewpoints) about how the world operates that play in your head each time you encounter an 'As it is.'

*I used to own an indoor climbing wall and one day a young, fit-looking, couple came in with their children and said that they wanted them to climb. I asked the parents if they would also like to climb. Instantly they declined my offer, having happily agreed to send their children up the climbing wall. I pressed them a little further, pointing out how safe it was, how all the climbs conveniently started at ground level, and how lots of other parents climbed with their kids. Still the answer was "No" because, and this is the crunchy bit, they said "I cannot see myself doing that" and, if you cannot see it you cannot do it.*

*Later, a mother in her forties came in with her son and when I asked the same question, she was a bit surprised because she hadn't intended to climb.*

*She said that she wasn't especially fit and had never climbed before but would like to give it a go! She could see herself doing it. She had a great time and climbed really well.*

## Changing your filters

Changing filters can be a lengthy process involving the imprinting of new ways of thinking, usually achieved through meditation. The aim is to alter our thinking at a deep level by focusing on what we really want to believe. In essence, it comes down to a struggle between our rational, thinking self and our unconscious (emotional) self, which comprises our filters. We like to think that our rational self is in control of how we operate, and that what we think is a useful way of behaving is how we will actually behave. In reality, our filters drive our behaviour.

## The rider and the elephant

In his book *The Happiness Hypothesis*, Psychologist Jonathan Haidt likens the struggle between our rational mind and our unconscious (emotional) mind to that of a rider on an elephant, with the rider being our rational mind and the elephant our unconscious mind. There is an old joke 'if an elephant wanders into your bedroom where does it sleep?' the answer to which is 'anywhere it likes.' The joke captures the reality of how deeply-held beliefs (our unconscious mind), rather than our rational wishes, ultimately drive our behaviour.

Our filters are operating all the time, whether we like it or not, and we are quite unaware of most of them until they present themselves. Once triggered, filters are usually felt as a physiological change such as becoming angry, agitated, feeling 'down', or perspiring.

Long term you are faced with a choice of either doing something about a filter that you are finding unhelpful or repeating the same experience. Having said that, if you react negatively to snakes but are unlikely to encounter one, you may consider it not worth doing anything about it choosing instead to accept the situation and move on.

**What to do**

To change your behaviour, you can either carefully train the elephant (change your recording) so that it behaves in the way you want, or you can distract it (seize the moment) when it is about to do something about which you are not happy. This ongoing struggle explains why, time and again, very senior and important public figures behave in ways that seem inexplicable and totally contrary to their long-term interests.

## The role of meditation

Trying to change deep-seated filters (train the elephant) while you are in 'busy-busy' mode rarely works because the logical part of your brain counters any new idea with "Nah! I don't think so. That is the way it is and nothing is going to change it." One way of dealing with this, so that you do not keep on racing around the same unhelpful self-fulfilling cycle, is meditation.

Meditation quietens the mind to the point at which it can entertain the possibility of exploring and adjusting its view of the world. Sometimes a change in viewpoint can come in the twinkling of an eye, as with one of life's shocks; other times it can take twenty or thirty days of considered contemplation.

*A good example of people suddenly changing occurred at the start of a workshop. As a result of a serious and long-standing disagreement, two directors came to see me and asked if the workshop would fix their dysfunctional working relationship. I pointed out that I was not in the business of directly fixing people's problems but encouraged them to come along and, without any particular expectation on their part, reflect on their situation as we covered the various topics. Two hours into the first day, and shortly after we had explored the self-fulfilling cycle, one of them came up to me in a break and said "It's all sorted!" I was somewhat surprised by this sudden change of heart and asked what had happened. He replied that while exploring the self-fulfilling cycle he had suddenly seen how he had been contributing to what was happening. He said that, in a Zen-like moment of enlightenment, he had seen things for what they were. As a result of this insight the pair was able to work out a long-lasting and amicable solution. All they needed was the opportunity to view their situation in a new light and the courage to create the change; what happened is not especially common but it pays to be open to the unexpected.*

There is no shortage of information on how to meditate so I will leave further exploration of this topic as something for you to follow up.

*Changing a filter is a choice which once made can deal with a situation forever*

## A note on 'should'

Sometimes people express concern about having to adopt some standard filter or other, or that they may turn into clones. This is not about filters that you should or should not have. 'Should' comprises someone else's expectations about how you need to behave. When it comes to filters, we have millions of them operating; some are helpful and others are not. It is entirely up to you to decide which to enhance and which to discard. The helpful filters take you forward; the unhelpful ones hold you back. You know them when you run into them.

*Beware that you are not 'Should' upon by others*

## Second opportunity—seize the moment

The second opportunity for change allows for immediate action but requires effort on each occasion that a situation arises. For instance, if there is a manager that you cannot stand but are required to work with, every time you deal with that person you will go into the same thinking loop. If you want to change the situation, you will then need to deliberately reset your thinking about the prospect of meeting with them. This is where the 'count to ten before acting' approach may come in. It creates a space in which to let go of your immediate feelings and consider ways of responding other than your first reaction.

As mentioned earlier, in the long run, changing the recording (filter) is easier and less painful than the second option of seizing the moment but it requires effort upfront. Then again, changing the recording saves you from having to constantly race around the same old track thinking in the same old unhelpful ways. When these filters are operating, we sometimes have the luxury of catching our self-talk, of reframing our thinking; other times we don't and go straight to creating the next unhelpful moment.

## The ultimate freedom

In his book *Man's Search for Meaning*, the eminent psychiatrist Viktor Frankl talks about his time in the Auschwitz concentration camps and what he came to see as 'the ultimate freedom.' He had many insights into the human condition but perhaps the most powerful was the realisation that he had the ultimate freedom of being able to choose his viewpoint. Even in the extreme conditions of the concentration camp he could choose to view his guards with anger, with pity, or with compassion. This was a major shift in his thinking.

## On making a decision

A senior manager told me that he had always thought that he could delay making decisions. He would say to others or to himself, "I will make a decision next month," until one day, in a blinding flash of the intensely obvious, he realised that he had just made a decision. His insight may seem obvious but it was a big change in his thinking. Likewise, your viewpoint is a choice; a decision that you cannot avoid making. This is why a statement such as "They made me angry" is the language of a victim.

> *The ultimate freedom is the freedom to choose—and doing nothing is a choice*

## Nature versus nurture

Frankl's notion of the ultimate freedom immediately touches upon the 'nature versus nurture' debate in which your behaviour is already determined, leaving you with little control over it. If you believe that you are who you are, and do what you do 'because it is in your genes and that is that' then there is little room for change. Any attempt to modify your behaviour would be wasted effort. However, current scientific research shows that the balance between nature and nurture is around 50/50 (which many suspected to be the case all along). This leaves plenty of room for improvement and takes away the excuse "There is nothing I can do."

As humans we can choose many different, and hopefully more constructive, responses to what we encounter as we travel through life; when and how we react is a choice not destiny.

> *It is not what happens that matters, it is how you respond to what happens*

## Can someone make you angry?

"Hold on," you say. "Of course someone can do something that makes me angry." Good point. They certainly did do something and you certainly did become angry. But did they *make* you angry? At some level it may seem as if the person really did make you angry but, if that is the case, the other person has power over how you feel. Is that something you want to accept?

"But," you say, "does it really matter if I say they made me angry? Surely it's just a turn of phrase, just words. I don't mean it literally." Well, yes it does matter and the thinking that gives rise to those words can lead to serious consequences.

> I was once invited to the Anger Management section of a prison where violent offenders were offered courses to help them manage their anger. The main room was large, open, light, and airy. Filling one of the main walls was a whiteboard and it was covered with 'feeling' words—happy, angry, relaxed, sad, thankful, surprised, and so on. I enquired what it was about and was told that many of the prisoners did not have a vocabulary with which to express how they felt; the closest that many could get to a 'feeling' statement was "You piss me off!" Also, they had no sense of being able to control their response. They truly believed that people made them angry and, in a weird reversal of logic, saw themselves as the victim because the other person had made them angry. Consequently, the other person deserved to be thumped; all very straightforward and as victims (in their world) their actions were justified. What we believe has consequences.

The language of victimhood can be replaced with language that reflects you taking responsibility for how you feel and operate. For example, "You made me angry" could become "I am angry about what you did." Looks similar to the first statement but is coming from the point of view of taking responsibility for how you feel. Moreover, when you deliberately choose "I am . . ." rather than "You made . . ." it forces a helpful internal dialogue about what is going on and how you feel about it.

## The effects of self-talk

You have many self-talks in a day and if amongst these internal dialogues you repeatedly use a phrase such as "They made me angry" it becomes something of a mantra and, at some deeper level, embeds itself in your filters. At this point you start to actually believe that they really did make you angry. Once this happens you have lost control of how you feel and become a victim, with the other person in control of how you feel.

The issue is not about whether or not you become angry; it is about not blaming others for you feeling angry, taking responsibility for how you feel, and acknowledging that how you feel is a choice not destiny. Any shift in viewpoint can be quite difficult because—

*What you learn depends on what you believe*

# The internal (eternal) struggle

It is your filters that prevent you from seeing what others see: things that may be tying you to the past. In the end, life really is an illusion, a compilation of petty grievances, slights, jealousies, hurts, sorrows, regrets and so on mixed with feelings such as love, compassion, kindness, humility, empathy, and optimism. Some see this in terms of an ongoing internal struggle, which raises the question of how to focus on and build our positive traits.

*An Indian elder, talking to his people about his own internal struggle, described it as a terrible fight between two wolves. "One wolf is evil, full of hatred, hurts, jealousies, anger, bitterness and lies; the other is good and full of love, humility, kindness, compassion, joy, and peacefulness."*

*"Which wolf will win?" he is asked.*

*"The one I feed," he answered.*

In a Zen moment, a friend memorably observed, "You know, if it wasn't for people in the world everything would be 'As it is'" and in that moment he captured it; problems do not exist out there, on their own. We create them in our head and then act accordingly. They are the result of our filters at work.

## The big picture

The Self-fulfilling Cycle operates on a small scale and also on a much larger one. Where you are in life is a combination of circumstance ('As it is') and the filters that you hold. Each time you are faced with making a decision, consider how it fits with the filters you want to nurture, whether it supports your future, or ties you to the past.

*On one occasion, I was booked to fly to a venue to lead a workshop. Before driving to the airport, I checked with the airline and was told that the flight departure time had been put back one hour due to a severe local storm. Leaving with plenty of time for the drive to the airport, I set off. But, shortly after getting on to the highway, I was suddenly faced with opposing traffic that was being rerouted onto my side of the road due to the opposing lanes being blocked by a landslip. This was not a good omen. Then the traffic crawled to a standstill and I was starting to visualise the workshop participants sitting there in silence waiting for me. I saw myself arriving flustered and ill-prepared, with things getting off to a wobbly start.*

*Fortunately, I caught myself creating these negative images and also noted that my heart rate was high. I decided to make a deliberate choice about how to view the situation; what would be would be, the airline would do its best, the venue owners would look after the participants, the participants would have time to relax and get to know each other, and there was nothing I could do to speed up the traffic. With these thoughts in my head, I deliberately sat back, relaxed, and enjoyed the drive through the stormy weather.*

*As luck would have it, I arrived at the airport in good time. But it was jam-packed with people from delayed flights. The automatic machine would not accept my e-ticket and when I got to the check-in counter, the woman, without even looking at me, stuck out her hand, waved her fingers, and asked for my papers.*

*Remembering my deliberate choice of mindset, I caught her eye and quietly observed that it looked as if she was having a hectic time. She looked up at me and said that the place had gone berserk and everyone wanted to be given special treatment. She also told me that the reason the machine wouldn't work was because my flight had been cancelled, and the next flight was three hours later. "Oh well," I said, "if that's how it is, that's how it is. It will all work out. Just do the best you can."*

*"Oh!" she said. "That is so sweet." This was not exactly how I would have described myself but I went with the drift. Then she gave me a big smile, said that she would try for another flight and asked if, in the meantime, I would like to use her phone to call the venue.*

*Short story: I got on the flight, arrived at the venue feeling relaxed and in good spirits to find that it had been set up exactly as I liked it, started on time with a lovely group of people, and we had a great workshop.*

## Scary creations

I started that journey by creating a hypothetical scene in my head. It wasn't real, but I was still getting agitated about it, and scared myself with what I had created, as if it had happened or was happening. I was then on my way to basing my next action on how I was feeling at that moment. Luckily, I changed the recording in time to save myself a lot of grief and was able to create a great day, storm or no storm. So the question of whether or not someone can make you angry is quite a big one.

# Tool 2

# Solve the 'blame equation'

## Your experience depends on what you believe

The 'blame equation' lies at the heart of Frankl's insight about the freedom to change your viewpoint: that we have a choice.

**The Blame Equation**

# Blame

## 'As it is' + filters = experience

*We tend to blame our experience on 'As it is' while ignoring the impact of our filters (beliefs/models/viewpoints)*

The equation highlights how easy it is to confuse what happens ('As it is') with what you experience. If you think back to the airport check-in story in the previous chapter, it is clear that the initial 'As it is' was not the sole determinant of my experience and that, by extension, solving the blame equation can make a big difference to what you experience.

> *A car suddenly changes lanes and cuts in ahead of you. You feel an immediate sense of annoyance at such inconsiderate behaviour. "What an idiot!" you say under your breath (you are most restrained . . .) and sound your horn to let the person know about your annoyance; after all, it is behaviour like that that causes road rage and all the other problems.*

Clearly, events or actions cannot be undone and what has happened has happened. It is 'As it is' but what if you knew that the passenger in the offending car had terminal cancer and was out for a last look around the city? It is likely that, in the light of the second scenario, you would have adopted a different, more forgiving stance than "They are either incompetent or did it to annoy me."

## Placing the blame

It is easy to place the blame for your experience on what happened while totally ignoring the part that your filters play in creating your experience. Yet your filters are the only part of the equation over which you have control. A ridiculous but rather common example that exposes the process is stubbing your toe on a chair and then swearing at the chair as if it was responsible for what had happened. The chair did not do it intentionally, it did not mean to do it and it was probably quite unaware of your existence.

Blaming the action or event for what we are experiencing assumes that the experience is inevitable and purely dependent upon what happened. This idea is strongly encouraged by the news media and others, with phrases like 'The whole country was shocked by . . .' as if there was only one response (experience) to a given event. The idea also applies to when we say to others something as simple as "That is really annoying." We assume (hope) that others are having the same experience and are equally annoyed but, by speaking on their behalf, we leave ourselves open to having our assumptions challenged, as in "I do not consider it at all annoying." Rephrasing the statement to "I am annoyed about that" means that you are speaking for yourself and your experience cannot be challenged because it is not a viewpoint or an opinion. It is simply 'As it is.'

## Speak for yourself

As a general comment, wherever possible, speak for yourself. That way you are on safe ground.

> *I was at a concert given by a small group of widely known and respected professional musicians. At the end of the concert, a person stood up to thank them and in her closing remarks said that "The group was very competent and played well together and they had done very well with one piece notwithstanding their remarks to the contrary . . ." Bear in mind that these were professional musicians. I immediately started to cringe, hoping that she would not go on in a similar vein but she did. The musicians managed to hold a fixed smile and we got through it but the comments were so inappropriate; far better for her to have owned her viewpoint by referring to how much she had enjoyed the concert, their particular style, and their choice of programme.*

## We always see (seek) evidence that supports our view

For instance, if someone has wronged you in some way and, because of that, you see the person who did it as being mean and untrustworthy, it is likely that from that point onwards, you will see them in the light of someone who is mean and untrustworthy. Even if the person comes on bended knee, apologises and offers a gift it will, in all probability, be seen as yet another example of the person 'crawling' or trying to 'get on the right side of you' for some ulterior motive.

The trouble is, unhelpful filters about a situation continue to tie you to the past and the stronger they are the more sure you will be that your viewpoint is the 'true' one. That is what makes Frankl's shift in how he viewed the concentration camp guards so remarkable. Frankl had every reason, and lots of examples, for holding to a view that the guards were sadistic brutes and that his view was the correct one; how could it be otherwise?

*One thing is certain, you cannot reach to the future with both hands hanging on to the past*

## End of the world versus drinks on the balcony

Through our filters, we zoom in on those actions or events about which we can say, "Ah ha! Told you! Just as I expected!" What we notice confirms our view of the world and those things that do not fit with this lopsided view tend to go unnoticed or are dismissed as irrelevant or untrue.

*I belong to a tramping club that owns a very nice lodge high up on the slopes of Mt Ruapehu, an active volcano that erupts every few years. One afternoon, Mt Ruapehu was having one of its occasional fits. Television news crews saw the event as a great opportunity to increase ratings by touching on many people's fears about possible harm and general fear of the unknown; aviation authorities warned of danger to aircraft; climbers on the top of the volcano viewed being pelted with rocks as a signal to quickly vacate the area; many farmers on land surrounding the volcano were concerned about the possibility of ash covering their property, and so on. Meanwhile back at the lodge, club members, with pre-prandial drinks in hand, were on the balcony observing the spectacle with considerable enjoyment, if not relish. Interestingly, there was no noise, just huge black clouds of ash being ejected high into the sky—a bit like TV with the sound turned off. It was very good.*

The event was the same, but the experience of the event depended on who was viewing it, the filters that they held and the scary scenes that they played out in their respective heads.

## We choose our response

The above story raises the issue of how to respond to an event or action over which we have no control, for example, an volcano erupting, being made redundant, our house burning down, the airline losing our luggage, or a flood blocking our way.

Some things we can change. Our curiosity and amazing capacity for invention can often help us to overcome many obstacles but what if we come across the immovable object, the erupting volcano, bankruptcy? What do we do when the expected or preferred veers away from what has actually happened? We are faced with making a considered decision: accept the situation or endeavour to alter it. The line between the two approaches can be a fine one and only you can decide which to take. What can be said is that railing against necessity or overwhelming odds, besides being futile, leads to frustration, unhappiness, personal turmoil, and illness. Stoicism has its place.

*In life, we are always subject to constraints, even though we would like to believe that we have complete freedom*

## A change of view

*A nurse told me about a time when she had to advise a woman, whose sister had been in an accident, that there was nothing more that could be done and that her sister was going to die. The woman became physically and verbally abusive towards the nurse, to the extent that the nurse was about to call security. Feeling quite threatened by the woman's behaviour, the nurse realised that she (the nurse) was sliding into an unhelpful Self-fulfilling Cycle. She managed to catch her thinking in time to step back outside the Cycle, see the situation 'As it is,' acknowledge how she was feeling, and then deliberately choose to view the woman as needing to be heard. The scene quickly changed and the nurse was able to be of much greater assistance.*

*What happens in life is 'As it is.' Our experience of life depends on our filters*

# Tool 3

# See other viewpoints

## First seek to understand

Of all the tools, seeing other viewpoints (listening) is possibly the toughest to apply and it is all to do with our filters.

### A matter of intent

When asked "What is the purpose of listening?" most people focus on the listener. They say things such as "The purpose of listening is to understand ... to act upon what is heard ... to correct misunderstandings" and so on. Pressed for more ideas, a significant shift usually takes place as they volunteer other purposes along the lines of ". . . to show respect" or ". . . acknowledge the other's viewpoint." The significant shift is that the metaphorical spotlight has moved from the listener to the speaker: from trying to find something out or wondering, "How do I respond?" to "What is this person trying to convey?" It is the acknowledging of this second part that makes listening so powerful and amongst the greatest services that one person can offer to another. Of course the listener may have to check if someone understands what they have been told or figure out how to respond to what is being said but far and away the most helpful purpose is that of being of service to the speaker.

*Listening is one of the greatest services that one person can offer another*

## A fraught process

You may have a concept or feeling that you want to share with someone or maybe you simply want to get something clear in your own mind. So far so good but, some time ago, in a blinding flash of the rather obvious, I realised that what we say is not necessarily an accurate representation of what is we have in our head—which is usually a picture! Words are simply code used to transmit our message to another. However, they are a poor approximation of what is going on in our heads and this makes getting your message across rather prone to error.

In the diagram below, the speaker is attempting to transmit a concept (in this case a wriggly shaped square) to the speaker, but the message that arrives in the listener's head ends up shaped as a triangle. This distortion is due to the effect of the two sets of filters plus the encoding and decoding of the message with each stage adding to the overall distortion. It is a source of ongoing wonder to me that an accurate facsimile of the original message ever gets across.

## A fraught process

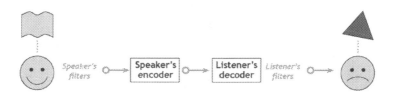

To get their message across, people use many different codes, such as Chinese, UK English, US English and so on, each offering an imperfect method for helping the listener to appreciate the speaker's unique (and I do mean unique) view of the world. It is bad enough that, even when fluent in a particular code it is, at best, far from perfect and that is without considering all the other factors contributing to the difficulties of accurately transmitting what is in your head.

For instance, the code used may not be your first language or your understanding of a word may be quite different to that of someone else. This is neatly summed up by the observation that England and the USA are 'two countries separated by a common language.' And if all that is not enough to create confusion, the speaker and the listener each have filters operating that load words with additional meaning in the form of historical and emotional baggage which, depending on how the parties are each feeling, varies from day to day. Bit of a miracle that we ever get anything across successfully! No need to travel to a foreign country for things to get lost in translation. Try talking to your local computer geek to sort out a smartphone problem.

## The art of listening significantly improves things

Imagine the situation in which the speaker has a smiley thought or concept in her head (a wavy square) and wishes to implant this in the listener's head. She chooses a code (say, English) and encodes her message through her filters. This leads to the first major opportunity to scramble the message because, as described above, the words we choose depend very much on how we are feeling as well as on our command of the language. The combined result of these two factors is that, on different occasions, we are likely to choose different words to describe exactly the same thing, which leads to the next difficulty.

The output of the speaker's 'encoding machine' is fed into the listener's 'decoding machine' thus creating a second major opportunity for scrambling the message. Here, the listener's machine is operated through his filters. Depending on his command of the incoming language (he may not be familiar with a particular word or English may not be his native language), and how he is feeling on the day, a word may appear to be especially loaded with meaning. He then reads the message in an entirely different light to that of the sender. This effect may be occurring now if you are having to reread this paragraph.

## Emails and texts

To illustrate the effect that filters have on how a message reads, think of a time when you have written an email late at night and then read it again the next day. It sure can look different "Whoa! That wasn't what I meant!" One 24/7-service organisation has banned the sending of emails (other than formal emergency emails) between the hours of 10 pm and 6 am because of the conflict they generate. Before the ban, operators would compose an email at 2 am and send them to people who would read them at 10 am. The difference between what the speaker implied (in the dim wee hours of the morning on sole watch) and what the listener later inferred (in the bright light of a new day) was considerable. Imagine how much more fraught a cryptic text message sent from your mobile would be.

With written messages we lose the usual visual cues that accompany what is being said and adjust our understanding accordingly. With only the bare text to go on our filters run riot looking for subtle meaning in the message. Given the right light, even the inclusion of a word as simple as 'Please' can take on a menacing tone. *"Would you please get the draft out on time . . ."* Recipient interpretation: "Please? What do you mean—please? I missed it just the once and now you put the heat on." On the other hand, the writer may have simply been taking take care to ask nicely.

Even with all the visual cues, unless there is some form of checking/feedback (listening), by the time a message has gone through the usual process and been implanted in the listener's head it is something of a miracle if it conveys the original idea. And that is without the usual additional distractions ranging from background noise to feeling hungry.

## The first person to become conscious

In the diagram below, the first pass through the process (solid arrows) resulted in a sad face on the listener whereas the speaker's intent was to pass on a happy thought. So when this happens, the question is "Whose responsibility is it to do something to correct the situation: the listener's or the speaker's?" To which the answer is "The first person to become conscious" and by 'conscious' I mean the first person to step outside the Self-fulfilling Cycle and acknowledge how they are feeling, because until this happens all parties remain trapped in the cycle. Of course this requires one person to leave the moral high ground of "If he cannot understand then that is his problem" and make the effort to rectify things.

## The process of listening

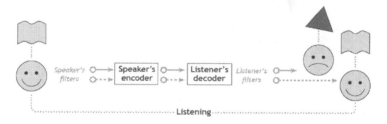

When things are going wrong, listening breaks the cycle by checking for understanding and then taking action to sort things out. In this case, let's assume that the speaker is the first to spot that the listener's reaction is out of keeping with the intended smiley nature of the message. The speaker might comment that she noticed that the listener grimaced at her comment, one that she had intended as a compliment. The listener explains why he reacted that way and then the speaker can have another try at getting the

intended message across (the path following the
dashed arrows). The speaker again checks to see if the
listener's understanding of the message is in line with
her view (as the author of the message) and if so all is
well.

If the listener had been the first person to 'become
conscious' then he could have carried out the same
process but in the opposite direction starting with a
statement such as "I didn't find that funny. What did
you mean?" And so on.

## Assembling the jigsaw

When helping to clarify and express what is going on
in a person's head it is as if you are helping them to
assemble a jigsaw puzzle. They have all the pieces but
they are not making a coherent picture. By encouraging
the speaker to explain what is going on—and
sometimes just shutting up is all the encouragement
that is required—the listener helps the speaker to
make sense of things and (often) form a view about
what to do next, all without any advice being given by
the listener.

Of particular note when listening is how the speaker's
ideas on what to do next are often quite different to
the advice that the listener would have offered had

they not held back. A common example of this is where someone drops into a colleague's office and asks, "Can I bend your ear for a moment or two?" At the end of the time they may get up to go and say, "Thanks for listening to me. That was really helpful," even though the colleague may have actually said very little other than to encourage the person to explore her or his own thinking on the matter.

**The relief of not having to come up with advice**

Focusing on helping others to clarify and express what is going on for them in their world relieves us of the need to offer advice. This is a blessing for both the speaker, who probably does not want advice, and for the listener who cannot possibly know which bit of advice will really fit the speaker's circumstances: the latter because we view the world through our own limiting filters and, even with careful listening, can only get a hazy glimpse of what is really going on for the other.

## Listening roadblocks

It is our filters that make empathetic listening difficult to do. I say 'to do' because listening is an activity that, generally speaking, requires effort rather than just passively soaking up whatever is being said. As we listen to someone's story, based on our experiences, we tend to project what we think is going to happen next and, even worse, start to think of ways in which the person could or should fix whatever is going on for them, all of which act as roadblocks to listening.

Many things are done that get in the way of tuning in to the other person's view of the world, things that shift the metaphorical listening spotlight from the speaker to the listener. Some roadblocks are mere annoyances; others stop the process in its tracks. Try these for a fit: staring over the person's shoulder, fiddling with a pen, sharing experiences, interrupting, thinking about dinner, offering advice, or asking questions to satisfy your own curiosity rather than to help the speaker further their understanding of what is going on. Of these, offering advice is perhaps the most common and also potentially the most disruptive, especially if it is unsolicited or just plain untimely.

There are times when sharing your own experience while the speaker is still explaining their story is entirely appropriate, such as when the other person starts to feel a little foolish and becomes increasingly hesitant about going on. Disclosing that you once did the same thing may help the speaker to feel more comfortable about retelling their story. In this situation, even though you have momentarily stolen the spotlight, it is with the sole intent of progressing the speaker's story. However, keep your story short and move the spotlight back to the speaker at the earliest opportunity—usually very shortly after you started.

Another common roadblock is where the listener constantly (or habitually) responds with "Oh, right!" or "I see," or a drawn out "Okay." By themselves the words are fine; the frustrating bit is when the listener never (well, almost never) asks a clarifying question or responds in a way that encourages the speaker to expand on what was said, either of which would demonstrate that they were actually processing what was being said.

## I understand exactly where you are coming from. Yeah right!

Another roadblock that can be particularly irritating (there is no shortage) is the 'I understand exactly where you are coming from/know what you are saying' variety. It comes in many forms and tends to trigger my uncharitable side which interprets it as code for "Would you mind shutting up because I have a much better and rather more interesting story." How can we possibly understand or know. Even if we have encountered a similar 'As it is' for example, a broken leg, our experience would certainly have been different because we each hold onto different filters. Even with careful, active, and empathetic listening the picture we create is still only a poor representation of the original held in the speaker's head.

If you think that you really do 'understand where someone is coming from' then surely it is better to demonstrate the fact rather than telling them that you understand. Try saying something along the lines of ". . . it sounds like (pithy summary that gets to the essence of the situation)." Over the years I have had lots of feedback on this matter and it is always about how annoying it is to be told by someone that they 'understand,' mainly because it is usually accompanied by behaviour that emphatically demonstrates the opposite to be true.

> *A Human Resources manager for a large hotel related to me how she was talking to a young woman in her early twenties. The conversation was going along well, with the young women acting bubbly and bright, when she suddenly volunteered that she was thinking of killing herself. Now that radically altered the course of the conversation. The women's demeanour had been quite at odds with what was going on for her and*

*the HR manager told me that she did not see the sudden shift coming. This serves to demonstrate how easy it is to assume that another's world view is the same as our own and to then act on that assumption by, for example, giving advice. By way of a footnote to this story, the HR manager had listened well to the extent that the woman felt that it was safe enough to disclose how she really felt. Nevertheless, the manager still needed to be ready for the unexpected.*

*Listening sees past our filters, quiets the little voice chattering away in our head, and focuses on the speaker*

## Let go of the need for perfection

I need to say at this point that perfection is not the aim; we all make mistakes. It is simply a matter of becoming aware of what is happening and then doing something about it. For example if you suddenly realise that you have stolen someone else's story by interrupting them mid-flight and are now busily relating your (better) story, you could retrieve the situation, and shift the spotlight back to the speaker, by saying something like "So, tell me more about what happened to you" or "It sounded as if you had quite a problem with . . ."

Spending time and energy mentally beating yourself up when you catch yourself putting up roadblocks is not productive; it is better to do something to correct the situation.

> *The difference between a good cook and a great cook is not about creating great meals without fail; it is about being able to recover when disaster strikes. I was making this point to a group when a person wryly commented, "Try recovering from burnt rice!" Quick as a flash, another member of the group, who happened to be a top chef, said, "Burn the fish and call it Cajun." His retort brought the house down and I rested my case forthwith.*

## Active listening

Active listening helps the speaker clarify and express what is going on for them. It takes effort and, far from being a desultory affair, can take a lot of concentration; indeed a long session of listening closely to someone can be quite tiring.

To help put this effort into perspective, here are actions (levels of engagement) that, in increasing order of effort on the part of the listener, contribute to active listening.

## Levels of engagement

## A couple of warnings

**First**, the above list is *not* some order of how to mechanically go about listening. The purpose of the list is to draw your attention to actions that require increasing amounts of effort. The order in which you apply the actions (skills) is entirely up to you. However, I would say that making yourself un-busy (new word) would be an excellent start. **Second**, the mere application of so-called listening skills does not in itself mean that you are listening well and, if applied inappropriately, the actions will likely have the opposite effect. A simple example of this would be when someone, demonstrating their freshly-honed encouraging skills, constantly says "Aha!" or "Right" in response to every utterance from the speaker. At this point if the listener were to ask the speaker "What is it that's annoying you?" the likely answer would be "You constantly saying 'Aha'!"

## Seven levels of engagement

Well here we go—seven levels of increasing engagement that encourage the listener to convey what is going on for them.

### 1. Be un-busy

Stop what you are doing, divert your desk phone, place your mobile in a bucket of water, turn off your computer screen. Really! How hard can this be, yet so many people do not do it. They continue writing reports, picking up the phone when it rings, tapping away at their keyboard and so on.

> *Case in point: I went to meet with the manager of a facility on personal business. Having arranged the meeting time and duration in advance, I sat down in her office. She indicated that I start the discussion and politely asked if it was okay if she finished off some urgent photocopies while we talked. For some reason, I felt a bit of pressure to agree and it needed an effort on my part to*

*point out that what I had to say was important to me and that the copying would be a distraction. She quickly agreed and sat down and we had a productive meeting. But if I hadn't acted she would have carried on copying but maybe not listening.*

## 2. Be ready

In showing a readiness to listen we need to make a more conscious effort than being un-busy and demonstrate that the person has our full attention. This might involve moving from behind your desk to one corner or even moving to a coffee table or some other location that is less distracting.

## 3. Be encouraging

Minimal encouragers comprise subtle, and not so subtle, actions that demonstrate that the listener is in tune with what the speaker is saying. (Everyone does this to some degree often without even being aware of it.) These movements or sounds, when done appropriately and in tune with what the speaker is saying, indicate to the speaker that you are paying attention. The action may be a slight nod of the head, a smile or a quiet 'mmm'; at the very least, they indicate that there is 'someone home' taking an interest.

The effect of encouragers is considerable. Imagine a presenter standing in front of a group that is sitting totally expressionless, motionless, silent, offering no acknowledgement let alone applause. Without any feedback from the group, unless the presenter is of a particularly tough disposition, their self-talk will slowly take over. "They are looking bored. I must be boring. This isn't working. It must be the . . ." A quick way to kill a presentation.

If sometimes you are not really listening and are merely 'going through the motions' hoping that it will give the impression of listening, then you are likely to be caught out, or even worse, get badly off-side with the speaker and this includes phone conversations. Think of a time when you have absent-mindedly responded to a significant other, having picked up the phone while finishing off an important task. If your responses are not appropriate to the moment, or not in sync with what is being said, you will soon get a "You are not listening to me" (especially if the person can hear you tapping away on a keyboard).

## 4. Use Starters/developers

Sometimes the listener may need to say something to put the speaker at ease, get the conversation started, or pick up the thread of what it is that the speaker wants to explore. Questions such as "What has been happening?" help the conversation along while keeping it closely focused on the speaker. Starters and developers most often come in the form of questions, either closed or open.

## Asking questions is good

A key aspect of listening is the crafting and asking of questions but there is a sort of cultural taboo around asking a question of someone while they are talking, especially if the person is in full flight so to speak. There is also a worry that by asking a question it might reveal that you have missed something and will look a bit silly. The bad news is that if you have missed something and start to listen really carefully in the hope of picking up the lost information, such as a name, you are so focused on this task that you start to miss what is being said right now. It gets worse because now your self-talk is screaming "I've not only missed the stuff covered at the beginning of the conversation, I'm missing what she's saying now" and so on, until you crash and burn. Sound familiar?

## Beliefs around asking questions

The attitude to asking questions strikes me as intriguing because, for over twenty five years, I have discussed this matter with groups who have experienced high quality listening: listening in which questions are asked as a matter of routine. When asked how they felt about being interrupted by someone wanting to ask a well-considered question—and by well-considered I mean one focused on assisting the speaker to explore or develop their topic—the feedback has been unanimous; people really appreciate being asked questions. They treat it as a sign that the person is taking a close interest in what is being said with the speaker's self-talk being along the lines of "Wow! He is so interested in what I am saying that he is even asking questions to clarify a point." This result flies in the face of most people's intuition, which tells them that they might be seen as rude or uninterested. The key lies in the intent; the question needs to be focused on assisting the speaker to develop their thinking and understanding, not on the listener's own curiosity or agenda.

## Closed questions

Usually only requiring a brief often yes/no response, closed questions do not encourage the speaker to explore the topic further. They are a useful way of helping the speaker to arrive at a metaphorical fork in the road and choose which conversational path they wish to follow. However, the use of several closed questions in a row is a sure indication that the listener is likely following their own agenda (probably to satisfy their own curiosity) to guide the speaker to a particular conclusion. A great example of this was when I heard a well-known radio interviewer ask ten closed questions in a row. Clearly the interviewer had an end point in mind where, having backed her prey into a corner, she could finally say "Gotcha!" This is not listening.

## Open questions

On the other hand, open questions require longer and often more considered replies than closed questions. Well applied, open questions encourage speakers to explore their thinking and reach their own conclusions. In the example described above it would have been far more interesting if the interviewer had used plenty of open questions to draw out and reveal the interviewee's views on the subject instead of our having to see everything through the interviewer's filters. The listeners can then make up their mind as they see fit.

You have doubtless heard of the famous five Ws: What, When, Who, Where, and Why. Words that, when used to start a question, usually result in it being open (although with a little work it is still possible to twist the sentence around to make it closed again). For example "Where did it happen?" "How does this fit with your situation?" "What is your view on this?" The first four Ws keep people firmly in the present. The exception to this, unless used wisely, is 'Why.'

Why, you may ask. Well, I was sitting in a café with a friend and feeling decidedly angry (but not with my friend) when, wanting to be helpful, he enquired "Why are you angry?" My instinctive reaction was along the lines of "If I understood why I was angry, I probably wouldn't be angry." I did not find the question at all helpful, even though it was well meant. The difficulty with the 'Why' question is two-fold; it can sound quite accusatory as in "Why did you do that?" or it can sound therapeutic, sending the recipient into the past and proffering "Well, it all started when I was three months old . . ." at which point you may need a couch for one of you.

In both cases, the effect of the question is like a blow to the side of the head with the speaker being knocked off the conversational track, eyes glazed, searching around for an answer and you possibly needing to come to the speaker's aid. After all, it was the question that knocked the speaker off their train of thought so maybe the least you can do is help the person to get back on track. A starter, such as "Tell me more about when the process was first set up" can get things rolling along again.

But do not despair! 'Why' does have a role to play. Take the situation where someone has been going on for twenty minutes without any sign of reaching a conclusion. Asking a question at this juncture such as "Why are you keeping it going?" may stop them in their tracks, causing them to review the situation or reassess their position.

'Why' questions are tempting throwaway lines. They can be used with little thought making it easy to become lazy in our listening practices. Someone once commented that "When you own a hammer, everything can look like a nail" and so it is with 'Why.' It can look suitable for every occasion but you do not have to use it all the time. Short story: used deliberately, with care, with forethought, and infrequently, 'Why' does have a place but it can be a bit of a showstopper for a person in full flow trying to express what is going on in their head.

## 5. Check your understanding

As covered earlier, saying that you understand is worse than meaningless. The statement conveys nothing other than a clear message that in the absence of actions to the contrary you most likely have not got a clue: much better to demonstrate that you understand.

Having said that, this part is quite straightforward and is simply a matter of creating a space in which the listener and speaker can resolve any misunderstandings or misperceptions. Using summarising and paraphrasing of key points and asking clarifying questions you can check your understanding of the speaker's story and fix it correctly in your head. No assumptions and no need to say "I understand."

By the way, acknowledging another's viewpoint is not the same as agreeing with it but the two are often confused. Sometimes, acknowledging another's point of view can feel as if we are giving in, especially if we are the subject of criticism. (The last thing we want to do is validate the criticism—our filters at work again.) Yet the person holds the viewpoint whether we like it or not, so we may as well ensure that we fully understand it. Even though your filters may be screaming "Not so!" at you, acknowledge.

Acknowledging by saying something along the lines of "From what you are saying, it sounds like . . ." gives you time to think and demonstrates to the other person that they are being listened to. Later if you feel it necessary to provide a considered rebuttal, you will be well prepared.

## 6. Capture the essence

Capturing the essence is that moment at which, having listened carefully to the speaker's story, you succinctly reflect back what you have heard expressed. Not some boilerplate response, rather an intuitive leap to a short, coherent sentence that captures the totality of what the speaker has expressed in both words and body language.

> At a workshop, I happened to be nearby when one participant was telling the other about his soccer playing, how he wanted to play representative soccer, practised three times a week at night, played on the weekend and so on. At the end, the person listening observed, "It sounds like soccer is a big part of your life." The speaker, not having used those words at all during the conversation, was visibly taken aback by the clarity of the statement, confirmed that it really was a big part of his life and that, up until then, he had not fully recognised it as such. Clearly the listener had been listening and had captured more than just the words as spoken.

Another example could be someone saying that they are okay while constantly rapping their knee with their fingers. In this case the essence could be along the lines of "It sounds like . . . is having a major impact on your life." Far from a hit, miss, try again affair, you may only get one chance to get this part right otherwise you risk annoying the listener by demonstrating that you have not been listening.

## 7. Clarify the problem

Notice that this is the last step. There is no step 8 and in particular, no 'Give Advice.' This is it. The end. What a relief. No need to think up some clever idea or other, just one task: to help the speaker become clear about what the problem is, which we will cover in 'Clarify problems (p81)'. Sorry about the wait. However, you could jump ahead and read it now. It's okay.

Incidentally it often happens that, after some careful listening, the speaker comes to the conclusion that the situation that they were discussing is not actually a problem. This is not to say that they are suppressing it, just that it no longer has a hold on them and they have let it go.

## Being 'present' when least inclined

There are a couple of things to bear in mind here.

1)  You do need to want to listen, to be present. There is little point in pretending to be listening when you are just plain uninterested. It does not work for either party.

2)  You will feel least inclined to listen when you most need to. It is easy to listen when you are not the subject of the conversation but the moment you feel as if you are under personal attack it becomes really difficult to respond appropriately. Your filters are going flat out reacting to what is being said. Your own agenda takes over with self-talk such as "How dare she say that." Dealing with this is the real test.

A cautionary note: sometimes careful listening is proposed as the answer to everything whereas it is definitely not a sure path to an amicable relationship. Indeed it may expose the true nature of the gulf between the parties but at least they will know where they stand and can act accordingly.

*A community worker told me of a time when she visited someone who had recently suffered the death of a partner of many years. She sat there quietly for three hours with barely a word being exchanged then, as she got up to leave, the bereaved person reached out and thanked her for listening.*

# Tool 4

# Explore the problem-solving journey

The journey starts with a problem, which is seemingly obvious but, if you think about it, we cannot start the journey without a problem. Initially, at least, we do not choose problems; they simply present themselves unbidden and arriving when least expected. We cannot dream a problem up; we either have one or we don't, so starting out on the journey is not a matter of choice, rather a matter of how we travel along it.

## See it as a journey rather than a switch

Moving from the moment when you first realise that you have a problem to the moment that you have resolved it is a journey rather than a switch. With a switch you simply move from one state to another—now you have a problem, now you don't. Problem solving is a journey with many steps to consider, each offering an opportunity for you to influence what is happening: a major plus because you can take control.

Of particular note are the diverging and converging sections of the journey. With divergent thinking you are in 'exploring mode' seeking to understand what had happened, what the contributing causes were (the 'As it is') that led to the main event. The transition from divergent to convergent thinking is sudden; you can almost feel people's minds slam closed as they lock on to a favoured course of action. The danger is that we do not spend enough time in the first section and end up choosing a solution that is not appropriate for dealing with the problem.

## The journey

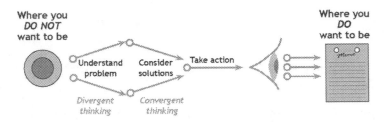

## Knowing is not understanding

Knowing that you have a problem is not the same as understanding it. For instance, if someone was hitting you on the head with a blunt instrument (assuming that you were not a masochist), you would probably find the resulting headache, lumps and associated side effects to be somewhat unpleasant. Clearly you would be aware that you had a problem but it is unlikely that, at that moment, you would understand it: why the person was hitting you on the head, what they were hitting you with, how long they would go on hitting you, and so on. The understanding comes later.

Think back to a time when you knew that you had taken one of life's big hits, one that left you feeling as if you had been punched in the stomach. First off, you did not need to wonder whether or not you had a problem; secondly, at that moment you would not have fully (and possibly not even partially) understood it. I am thinking here of understanding what you were experiencing: the hurt, anger, and so on. As we covered earlier, what you experience depends on what you believe which explains why the understanding comes later. It may take many days to really get to grips with what is going on. Problems cast big shadows (stress), hence the 'lie awake at 4 o'clock in the morning' moments and, even though we may not fully understand what is going on, defining a problem is a huge step towards reducing its shadow, to the extent that sometimes the problem just fades away.

The ability to define a problem is a skill that can profoundly influence how you operate and your well-being which is why it is the focus of its own chapter.

## Problems are treasures. "Oh noooo! Here comes the corporate speak."

I happily use the word problem rather than situation, opportunity or matter, because what we are dealing with is a problem and the other words are simply euphemisms serving to avoid people being seen to be associated with a problem. I mean, if it isn't a problem then why are we spending time on it!

In Japan, above the main building of a large manufacturing facility, I saw an equally large sign saying 'Problems are treasures.' Having suffered extensive bouts of corporate-speak from many years in the corporate realm, I promptly felt inclined to stick my fingers down my throat. However, once the concept had been carefully explained to me, I slowly came to realise the sign's true significance; if you cannot identify problems then you are stuck in the present. Everything is okay, nothing to do, until the rest of the world sweeps past.

Problems present the opportunity to create improvement and the more problems you identify and resolve the faster you improve. In this light they are veritable treasures. Mind you, one colleague, who at that moment had not fully bought into the treasure philosophy, declared that if problems were treasures then he was working in the treasury. We will ignore that comment.

> *A long time ago, I used to go around assessing supplier quality management systems: a process that could range from a few hours to several days. What I quickly discovered was that within minutes of arriving at a site I would have a pretty good idea of how long I would be there. In some cases I would be greeted by a management team that openly talked about problem areas, explained how they had established project teams to work on identified problems and how they were monitoring other processes looking for variance, and so on. I would set aside a few hours for the assessment. In other cases I would be greeted by a line manager assuring me that everything was under control and that there were no significant problems—it was all good: time on site, three days.*

In this second case, the managers were unaware of what was happening in their processes, assumed that no news was good news and treated the status quo as satisfactory—the 'if it ain't broke don't fix it' approach. In the first case, the management team were acutely aware that everything they did could be improved and saw problems as the gateway to improvement and consequently to be valued or treated as treasures.

Two philosophically opposed mindsets: one locked in the present, the other focused on continuous improvement.

## The problem-solving journey

Here is the journey (process) again, this time with a bit more detail. The problem, where you do not want to be, is dealt with in detail in the next chapter.

### The problem-solving journey

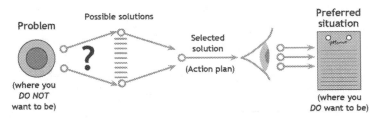

The journey has a number of key areas:

a)  Identification of the problem. People have great difficulty with this area yet it forms a large part of the journey.

b)  Divergent thinking to understand the problem and develop a list of possible solutions.

c) Convergent thinking to narrow the list of possible solutions for resolving the problem and then select the preferred option.

d) An action plan for implementing the chosen solution. People take to this part with great gusto and have little difficulty with it.

e) A description of the preferred situation or outcome that you would like to achieve. For instance, you might describe your preferred situation to be: working with a great team, doing what I enjoy, working in the outdoors, financially independent, opportunity to travel, drop in stress.

Although I have listed the stages of the process in a neat and tidy manner showing a logical progression, life is rarely like that. What actually happens is we tend to jump around somewhat. So I am going to imitate life and explore the various stages in a different order. I will also add a few other relevant comments and pull the whole thing together at the end of the chapter. I trust that you can bear with me in this.

## Deal with the urge to jump in with a solution

As I mentioned at the beginning of the chapter, the point of being aware that problem solving is a process is to reveal the many ways in which you can tackle a problem and avoid the pitfalls that await you: not to burden you with yet another clever chart.

One such pitfall is the urge to propose a solution; possibly because it is seen as being proactive but I think mainly because we seem to be hardwired to look for, and implement, solutions rather than clarifying what the problem is (that the proposed solution is supposed to solve). The usual result is a headlong and enthusiastic rush to implement a solution, and one that may not turn out to fit the problem.

## The danger of not understanding the problem

*In Borneo there was a serious outbreak of malaria and the World Health Organisation (WHO) immediately sprayed the area with dichlorodiphenyltrichloroethane (DDT) to kill the mosquitos that were spreading the disease. The malaria died down but, unfortunately, the DDT had also killed a parasitic wasp that lived off a caterpillar that, without the presence of the wasps, promptly started to eat the thatch-roofed houses, causing them to collapse. In addition, the DDT also killed lizards, which killed the cats that ate them, which allowed the rats to flourish, which led to an outbreak of sylvatic plague and typhus at which point WHO stepped in to resolve the new crisis by parachuting in more cats!*

*The problems that you are wrestling with today could be the outcome of solutions implemented yesterday*

Unless they have sat down and had a "Let's agree what the problem is" conversation, people instinctively jump in at the action plan point ignoring the less obvious questions, "What is this solution the answer to?" or "What will change?" I have yet to find an individual who, having become aware of a pressing problem, has sat down to consider the question "What is the problem?" This is not some throwaway line; it is a purposeful consideration of "What is happening about which I am unhappy?" My greatest difficulty is that of helping people to let go of their favourite solution, step back and have a look at what it is that they are trying to fix with their solution.

Although they have not defined the problem, people are ready to stoutly defend their solution. Think back and you will doubtless have heard a person or group boldly state that the problem is the failure to implement 'X' which is often (if not usually) the person or group's favourite solution: more on this in the next chapter 'Reducing the shadow.'

Groups are particularly prone to quickly locking on to the need to come up with a solution, possibly because they want to be seen as being proactive and looking to the future rather than dwelling on the past. But this might be a case of more haste with less speed.

## The importance of letting go

Let us imagine that you are in a room, that you are finding it to be very unpleasant and want to move somewhere else. At this juncture I might ask, "Where would you like to be?" To which you might reply, "Anywhere but here. This room is so awful. I just want out." Now, if you do not know where you are going, how can you get there? For instance, I might offer you a very nice room in New York, or the Antarctic, or perhaps next door. Each of these possibilities would get you out of the current situation but each would require a different action plan and would deliver quite different experiences. The point is that although you may have a morbid fascination in focusing on the current situation (think about how much time and brain space problems take up), until you lift your head (bit like a meerkat) and look to where you want to be, you are likely to remain trapped in your current situation. There is also the possibility that you could inadvertently break out and end up in an even worse situation.

## Prising your hand off the problem

A major problem can readily take on a life of its own, totally consuming your thinking, resources and energy.

*My wife and I lost a huge amount of money (all our life saving plus a lot more) in a business that we bought. We were haemorrhaging money at such a rate that there was no way that we could sustain it and things looked grim. Even worse, the problem was mesmerising us to the point at which we could not look to the future; we were fully focused on the bleakness of our current situation and pouring all our energy and money into it. Fortunately, a good friend, who is also a good listener (good example of the power of listening), helped us to gradually acknowledge (see) what was happening and then to lift our heads to describe where we wanted to be.*

*The simple action of prising one hand off the past freed us up to grasp the future; it was a lifesaver and in saying that I am not being trite. The shift in focus was huge because up until then, we had invested so much time and money that we did not want to let go of the situation and see it for what it was. The result of our new-found clarity was that we stopped what we were doing and crystallised our losses so that, instead of having in effect a moving target, an open-ended financial drain, we now had a fixed target. More importantly, having accepted what had happened and stopped it, we were freed to firmly focus on the future and create what we really wanted.*

The end point of that story is that the moment we started putting our energy into our preferred situation things started to turn around and we were soon on track to doing what we enjoyed.

## Let go

Failure to let go of the problem is common. People think that by working harder on whatever it is, things will get better but if it has not worked up to now, it may be time to acknowledge that fact. Having done that, you are then positioned to grasp the future. In business speak this approach is referred to as cut your losses and ride your successes. Trouble is, in real life those filters get in the way again—pride, attachment and so on. This is one of the most difficult lessons to learn: intellectually rather obvious but wait until it happens for real. As I mentioned earlier, it is difficult to grasp the future when both your hands are (grimly) holding the past.

## Be clear about your destination

Having listened for some time to a senior manager talk about a particularly stressful situation, I asked what she would prefer the situation to be. The question proved to be a real showstopper, causing her to pause as she thought through this unexpected question. She had become so immersed in the past and present that she had not given any thought to the future. This is not uncommon with people as they become transfixed by, and drawn into, what is happening or has happened, along with the attendant hours of '4 o'clock in the morning' rumination. On that point, if your lawyer presented you with a bill for five hundred dollars for legal work, plus a thousand dollars for worrying about it, would you pay the thousand dollars?

## Beware confusing your solution with your preferred situation

By clearly describing your preferred situation (where you want to be/the outcome you want) you are able to see if a particular solution is going to get you there and that it fits.

For instance, you might (among other things) describe your preferred situation as: financially independent, relaxed, doing a job that you enjoy and working in a friendly environment. This description will immediately focus your mind on those ideas (solutions) that will take you in that direction. So often I have seen people who, having got themselves into a very stressful situation, do things that add to their stress such as reignite an argument that has long passed or continue to describe someone in abusive terms referring to them as 'a . . .' You might experience some immediate gratification but, long-term, has the action contributed to where you want to be? Having a well-defined preferred situation enables you to align your behaviour by asking questions such as "How will this (action) contribute to where I want to be?"

## Problem solving in action

So, the real-life sequence of events is:

### The problem-solving journey

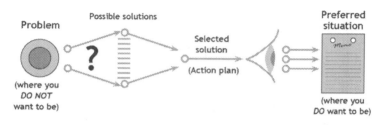

1) Define your problem (subject of the next chapter).

2) Look to where you want to be (your preferred situation).

3) Explore the problem so that you understand it and are then able to assess whether or not the selected solution fits.

4) List a range of possible solutions.

5) Select the solution that looks most likely to both deal with the problem (current situation) and deliver your preferred situation.

6) Develop and test your action plan (your chosen solution).

Whenever following the problem-solving journey be sure to always follow the **first four steps** in sequence: after that feel free to dance around wherever. At the end of the book there is a list of questions that can be used to guide you through the process.

**Cautionary note**

If you mentally step back when problem solving, you will notice that nearly everyone starts at the 'Action Plan' stage, usually with a statement along the lines of "You know, what we need is a new photocopier" (favourite solution to an undefined problem). This is because our overwhelming tendency is to jump straight to a fix and then argue its merits compared to someone else's fix of get it repaired or whatever. The trick is to recognise that this is happening and gently take yourself, or others, back to the start of the journey with a question such as "If we did that, what would change?" The answer to that question will get people describing the problem.

## The risk of losing the gem

Having listed a range of possible solutions—I am thinking of a list of at least twenty or more—and considering which option to go with, be careful not to ignore the possibility that there might be a little gem buried in there somewhere. Again, because of the keen desire to get to the finish line, people tend to look at the list and say something like "Look, in reality, there is only one practicable solution" with the resultant overlooking of a potential solution that may have been both inexpensive and quick to implement.

## The distraction of the big ticket solution

Sometimes, the gem solution is lost due to a focus on big ticket solutions because they look impressive and all that resource 'will surely do the job.'

> *An executive group working on a big problem nearly lost their gem solution. They had quickly decided that the best solution was a huge database; they had the resources to easily do the task but it would have taken about six to twelve months. After a bit of work on understanding the problem, becoming clear on where they wanted to be, listing and exploring a wide range of other options, they discovered that the best option was to place a*

*strategically positioned whiteboard in their main project centre. Moreover, they could implement the solution almost immediately at little cost. It got even better; using large sheets of newsprint as an interim measure, they could start immediately and refine the idea. It was a real eye-opener to see the shift from a project requiring a lot of money and time to such a simple solution.*

*In another case, a very senior group comprising the managing director, members of the board, and the executive group, started listing possible options (solutions) to resolve an IT problem within their company. The list included yet another huge IT project plus other expensive ideas until they reached the eighty-second idea on their list; tap into the same system developed and operated by (a sister company). All along, the group, which included the CFO (who was notoriously tardy when it came to spending money), had settled enthusiastically on the huge IT project as the answer so it came as a massive surprise when the eighty-second idea was put forward; a solution ready and available at minimum cost.*

Such is the power of jumping to a favoured solution and heading for the finish line, thereby likely overlooking the most appropriate solution.

## Tunnelling

Near the other end of the journey we have the business of the Action Plan with a variation on the rush to the finish line. What happens here is that, having chosen a course of action (solution), everyone is keen to get on with things. Metaphorically speaking, the hard hats are on, the bright lights are burning and everyone is working overtime, so lookout the person who suggests that there might be a better way of proceeding. Carrying on with the metaphor, the tunnel is going well, on time, within budget and right on course: a masterpiece of engineering. Now some bright spark comes along and suggests "If we had drilled fifty metres to the left of the current tunnel we could have saved a lot of time and money." Despite the merits of the proposal, the likely response from the project engineers would be the equivalent of "Please go away." The information has arrived too late and needed to have been sorted out earlier, in the exploratory stage.

### Tunnel features

- Once inside a tunnel it is not possible to see another tunnel. All you can see is the walls. Having committed to a course of action, it can be very difficult for people to change. Or more likely, having agonised over the first decision, they have little inclination to go back over old arguments.

- The only way out is backwards and no one likes going backwards.

- When pushed to do better the urge/drive is to dig faster in the same direction because that is what we do best and have got used to.

The point of all this is that it stresses the importance of the early stages of the problem-solving journey; the very stages that tend to get scant attention and which people want to hurry through to get to the action bit.


## Problem-solving timeline: a speed illusion

When it comes to seeing the problem-solving journey as a timeline it looks quite different. The old approach to problem solving was to spend little, if any, time on understanding the problem. In fact, my experience after many years working in and with manufacturing, service, hospitality, and community organisations has been that they do not define the problem in a clear, succinct sentence. The overall result of not spending sufficient time understanding the problem is spending a lot more time fixing spin-off problems in the post-implementation phase; hence yesterday's solution, today's problem(s). This is illustrated below where two groups are compared: one (Group A) that spends little time understanding the problem and the other (Group B) that carefully assesses the problem and comes up with a solution that fits.

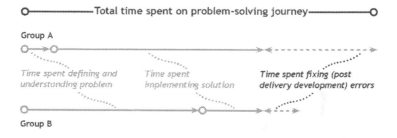

Notice how spending more time understanding the problem saves you time later—time spent fixing up the spin-off problems euphemistically referred to as post-delivery development. Although the need is not hard to grasp intellectually, the perceived pressure to deliver a result can make it very difficult to keep a group, and sometimes even yourself, focused on agreeing the problem and understanding it.

So there it is: a journey with plenty of opportunities to influence the outcome and create what you really want. However, beware the big trap: that of starting the journey with your favourite solution. When you do catch yourself starting with your preferred solution, ask the question "If I/we did that, what would change?" This will move the focus back to the start of the journey—the problem. Also, be sure to start by following the sequence of steps outlined earlier in the chapter—especially the first four.

# Tool 5

# Clarify problems

## Reducing the shadow

Problems can cast big shadows, often when we do not
even realise it.

> *At a workshop, a senior manager commented that*
> *he could not see the big deal about working on*
> *problems and that he did not have any to work on.*
> *I suggested that, as there was no pressure on him to*
> *find a problem, he might like to work with someone*
> *to help them explore what was going on for them.*
> *A little later, the same manager unexpectedly*
> *volunteered that he realised that there was one*
> *matter that, although trifling in nature, could*
> *possibly qualify as a problem. It transpired that, as*
> *a result of certain events that had taken place over*
> *a long period of time, he had decided that the best*
> *course of action to resolve things was to simply*
> *sell his house and shift himself, and his family, to*
> *another city. So here he was with 'no problems' yet*
> *ready to uproot himself and his family to move*
> *to another city to solve a problem that he said he*
> *didn't have. As the significance of his favoured*

*solution sank in, he started to realise that it may be worth spending a bit of time understanding what it was that he was unhappy about (the problem) to which moving to another city was the answer.*

## Stress and letting go

The aim of clarifying a problem is to see what it is that you are feeling stressed about, to reveal it, feel as if you can get your hands around it, acknowledge it for what it is, let it go, and then move on. When it comes to reducing stress levels, the ability to identify and understand a problem, involving as it does the letting go of the morbid fascination associated with continually rehashing it or ruminating over it, is of huge benefit.

## Vanishing problems

On many occasions, having defined a problem and seen it for what it is, without the attendant load of horse manure that often buries it, a person will decide that it is no longer a problem for them. It's not a matter of suppressing things; purely that the power that the situation once had over them has drained away. They realise that the situation is of no further interest and just want to let it go. Senior, highly experienced managers, having worked on defining quite a heavy problem, have come up to me to cautiously float the idea that what was a problem for them is no longer a problem. They ask "Is that okay?" and "Can we let it go?" as if it is up to me. This is another example of you being in charge. If your problem fades, that is it; no one else can decide the matter on your behalf.

Within our programme of three workshops, we have a 'Check-out' at the end of the first one at which we talk about how things are going and I ask each person "How is your problem coming along?" Now it is worth noting that, at this stage, the participants have not explored possible solutions to their problems, but the answers they give vary from "Nowhere near as big" to "Not a problem anymore." Bear in mind that many of these are not trivial matters and some people reported that initially they had felt physically sick about what had been, or was still, happening.

*Defining and understanding the problem is more than eighty percent of the journey*

## At the highest level

The highest level of active listening, that of clarifying the problem, is not about giving advice. In fact, giving advice does not figure at all. As mentioned earlier, done well, the clarifying of a problem dramatically reduces its shadow, sometimes to the point at which it disappears, which can come as quite a surprise to all concerned.

## Be advised

You may have noticed by now that I am somewhat circumspect about the giving of advice. This is because advice shifts the spotlight's glare firmly onto the listener who, although not actually listening at this moment, starts to act like an expert on the speaker's life. Of course there is a place for well-considered and sought after advice: but not at this moment.

A simple rule is to not give advice, even when it seems desperately appropriate, unless you have got the recipient's agreement. Furthermore, even if the recipient requests advice, it may not be appropriate to proffer it because, at that moment, you may not understand what it is supposed to fix.

## Making the problem clear

On 16 July, 1999 John F Kennedy (JFK) Jr. set off to pilot a light aircraft from Essex County Airport to Martha's Vineyard Airport off the Massachusetts coast. He had with him his wife Carolyn and his sister-in-law Lauren. Later that night, it was reported that the plane had disappeared with the loss of all on board and, over the next few days, it transpired that the plane had crashed into the sea.

During the course of the ensuing investigation, many factors emerged with regard to JFK Jr. and the accident. Here are a few.

1) **Recent licence**: obtained his Private Pilot's Licence just fifteen months prior to the crash;

2) **Weak ankle**: required assistance to operate rudder pedals due to ankle surgery six weeks before the crash;

3) **No Instrument Licence**: not licenced to fly in 'Instrument Conditions' of poor visibility or loss of horizon but allowed to fly at night in suitable conditions;

4) **Inability to see horizon**: weather fine but other pilots flying the same route reported visibility as '5-8 miles with haze and an obscured horizon'; at time of flight another experienced pilot declined to fly due to haze;

5) **Flew direct to Martha's Vineyard**: by opting to fly directly to Martha's Vineyard he had to fly over fifty kilometres of featureless open water rather than follow the coastline with its lights;

6) **Departed late**: originally intended to fly during daylight hours but Lauren's late arrival delayed the departure resulting in a night flight, and exacerbation of the haze and featureless water;

7) **Failed to file flight plan**: no one was aware of his intended route or estimated time of arrival;

   a) Psychological stress: marital problems—stayed apart from wife in hotel for three days prior to flight;

   b) during flight aircraft came 'uncomfortably close' to in-bound passenger jet forcing it to descend;

   c) his magazine 'George' was in serious financial trouble.

Now, as we explore what happened, you will see that it is a bit of a journey and, rather than jumping ahead, I would like you to hang in there and follow the plot. The sequence is deliberate and intended to get us to the point at which we can define what a problem is—any problem. Here we go.

First, give yourself time to digest the above points and then, without over analysing things, jot down your answer to the question "What was the problem?" A short, coherent sentence would do here.

For the sake of the argument, a typical answer to the above question (based on twenty-five years of working with groups) would be "His decision to fly directly to Martha's Vineyard over dark, featureless, open water at night." Now here's a mind twister for you. If indeed the problem was his decision to fly direct at night, then, if he had *not chosen* to fly over open water at night he would not have crashed. Of course the problem may not have been that but, if it had been, then it is reasonable to assume that not doing it would have prevented the problem. In this case, not crossing open water and instead following the coastline would, in all probability, have resulted in the aircraft arriving safely at Martha's Vineyard. To put it another way, what was proposed as a problem was, in fact, not a problem at all but a solution in disguise because it is implying that the sole cause of the crash was this decision. But what if a wing had fallen off? In this case it would not have mattered which route he had taken, the result would have been the same. The proposed problem (solution in disguise) would have then have diverted everyone's attention away from other possible solutions.

If the above is still not quite making sense, let go of it, and carry on reading. This is one of those situations in which the understanding gradually emerges from the gloom. At workshops, learning to define the problem creates more debate amongst the participants than any other point but, the overwhelming feedback is that it is also the most illuminating and powerful.

This is hard work so if it feels as if your brain is melting, do not fear; we are making progress. What we have discovered is that the proposed problem 'decision to fly direct . . .' has turned out to be a solution and not a problem after all and that can save a lot of wasted effort along the problem-solving journey.

*Most (nearly all) proposed problem statements*
*are actually solutions in disguise*

Now, cast your eye over the list of contributing factors and see if you can apply the same test of "If that was the problem then, would not doing it have prevented what happened." If the answer is yes then you have revealed another solution. Let us try another example:

'Weak ankle . . .' If indeed his ankle being weak had been the problem, then if his ankle had not been weak he would not have crashed. Therefore what had been proposed as a problem was actually another solution in disguise.

At workshops, disparate groups comprising line managers, scientists, directors, sales people, executive managers, and engineers offer the same result. After setting the scene, I ask, "What was the problem?" and am always presented with a list of solutions, plus the occasional outlier answer, to which I will return shortly. In the meantime—

> *When a sentence starts with 'The problem is a lack of . . .' you are about to be presented with someone's favourite solution or advice*

So in the search for the problem, the first thing we are able to do is eliminate solutions being put up as problems which shortens the overall list considerably, but we still have not defined the problem. I would like to leave this scenario for the moment to explore a few other points, after which we can have another look at this issue.

## Beware confusing your preferred situation (outcome) with a solution

Earlier, I mentioned outliers in the presented lists of possible problem statements. These tend to be statements of the rather obvious along the lines of "The plane crashed, three people died." Perhaps that is it; after all it does not leave much room for opinion. Now at this point you may be tempted to think that the opposite situation, in which the plane did not crash, is just another possible solution. Be careful, as it is another outcome, not a solution. It is easy to confuse the two but bear in mind **a solution is the means of getting from the problem to the outcome** and in this case the statement does not offer or even hint at a possible solution. It is a simple statement of fact; a statement of 'As it is'—plane crashed, three people died—and one that does not lead us anywhere. The 'As it is' statement has taken us another step forward but we have still not defined the problem.

## Thinking it through

Here is a thought puzzle for you to consider. An old but perfectly serviceable passenger jet is taken from a storage farm in the Arizona desert; there are so many aircraft there that one will not be missed. It is fuelled and filled with several hundred people who have no friends, no family and who, sadly, will not be missed either. (I know it is sad but steady on, it is only a mind game.) The plane crashes, unobserved, in a remote part of the planet. Everyone dies. Is it a problem?

The instinctive answer is "Of course, it must be a problem" to which I retort "For whom?" All the passengers died, no one observed it crash, no one will miss the passengers and the plane will not be missed. "Yeah," you say, "but it has to be a problem; you cannot have hundreds of people die without it being a problem." Mmm . . . Let us leave that thought hanging for a moment while we consider another scenario.

Several years ago, there was an earthquake in a remote area of Iran in which over fifty thousand people died. Without being too precious about it, was the earthquake a problem for you? I would suggest (and I realise that I am taking a chance here) that it is unlikely. Here we go again, fifty thousand people die and it is not a problem. Surely it must be a problem but what if a close friend of yours was travelling in the area at the time . . .

Your friend calls you the night before the earthquake to let you know that she is in the local village and plans to spend the next day looking around. Next morning, you hear on the news that a devastating earthquake has flattened the village and surrounding area. Is that a problem?

"Surely, yes," you say, "of course it's a problem."

"But why?" I ask.

"Because," you retort, "my friend may have been injured or killed."

So, what is the difference? Fifty thousand people die and it is not a problem: one person, who happens to be your friend, is possibly injured and that is a problem? The difference is that the possibility that your friend has been injured affects you directly whereas the other situation does not. (As an aside, if every event in the world was a problem then it is likely that we would quickly become suicidal under the unbearable load.) The two parts of seeing it 'As it is' plus connecting it to the effect it has on you pretty much defines what a problem is. Here is a statement that captures these points—

*A problem is an 'As it is'*
*that affects you negatively*

A dictionary definition of a problem is 'any thing, matter or person that is difficult to deal with, solve, or overcome.' The difficulty with that statement is that it focuses on the 'As it is' while ignoring the one thing that we can control—our reaction to what has happened ('As it is')—and that is where the 'affects you negatively' bit comes in.

## JFK Jr. scenario revisited

### Problem views

Going back to the JFK Jr. scenario there would have been many different problems surrounding the same central 'As it is' each having its own viewpoint. For instance, the makers of the aircraft would have been concerned about whether their aircraft had failed in some way, the dive salvage team would have had to consider the difficulties associated with a deep dive, the air traffic controllers would have been mulling over their part in the scheme of things and, of course, there would have been all the family members and close friends, each with a special viewpoint. In short, there are as many problems as there are people involved; each viewpoint is valid and people may sign up to help others deal with whatever the problem is for them. By way of an example, a problem statement for the aircraft manufacturer could have been "We are concerned that the aircraft may have had a crash-related safety defect."

*You can invite others to help you work on a problem but it is always, uniquely, yours*

## Avoiding the primordial slime

At this juncture, I need to point out that the purpose of the exercise is not to mystify but to reveal the essence of what it is that you are unhappy about. Clarifying the problem keeps you in the present moment, avoiding tracking back to the point where it all started. For instance, it may be that one day at work you need a special drawing pen only to be told that they are out of stock, whereupon you contact the wholesaler who tells you that the government has banned imports of that product and nothing can be done about it. Further investigation reveals that the whole thing is due to a UN agreement and on it goes until, eventually, you track your way back to the real source of the problem which was when we first crawled out of the primordial slime . . . You get the idea.

*A Problem is where you do **not** want to be, a Preferred situation is where you **do** want to be and a Solution is a possible means of travelling from one to the other*

At times it can seem downright impossible to nail the problem down. However, if you apply the earlier definition of a problem (an 'As it is' that affects you negatively) it could be that you were concerned that you would not get your work out on time which immediately opens up many alternatives for resolving the matter. You could use a different device, ignore the deadline, borrow a device, can the whole thing, try to get more use out of the old device, design a new approach and so on. It is so easy to get sidetracked and lose sight of the problem, the 'As it is' that is affecting you negatively.

## Moving problems

Many years ago, I worked for a manufacturing company and regularly ran into the 'moving problem' syndrome. I just could not figure out what the problem was so that we could all get down to working on it. Instead I found myself tracking things further and further back. Not only that, the things that people were offering as problems were usually their favourite solutions disguised as problems, as in "You know, the problem around here is that we never have enough staff . . ." It is so easy to get sucked in.

Once again, when you hear the words "The problem is . . . ." be on the lookout for an incoming solution.

## Crafting the statement

To define a problem well, we need a concise sentence.

- Avoid judging. 'He is lazy.' **Describe**. 'The report was not finished.'

- Avoid assuming. 'She knows what I mean.' **Clarify**. 'What is your understanding?'

- Avoid solving. 'The problem is that we haven't got the new computer.' **Seek to understand**. 'How do you see a new computer changing things?'

- Avoid labels. 'Sales people are like that.' **See the person**. 'Jo and Arnold are not happy with the new form.'

- Avoid generalising. 'You never/always . . .' **Be specific**. 'Give me a recent example of this.'

Let us see what this approach looks like in practice. Imagine that you are attempting to give feedback to a member of your team. Sitting opposite you, he is quiet, staring steadfastly at the floor while you talk.

What is the problem? Carefully think this through before you read the paragraph below. What would you say to the person?

Common suggestions are:

- He is not listening. (An assumption: how do you know that he is not listening? It may be his optimal listening stance.)

- He does not care. (Another assumption; he may care a lot but is scared.)

- He is lazy and does not want to know. (A judgement: lazy compared to whom?)

## A sample problem statement

A clear problem statement that meets the above criteria would be "X, I am finding it difficult to give you feedback while you are looking at the floor." This is 'As it is' plus your feelings. Once defined, a problem is glaringly obvious but sometimes, like the layers of an onion, it can take days to slowly strip away the steaming heap of judgements, assumptions, solutions, labels, and generalities under which we bury the 'As it is.' This is where the role of the 'Succinct, Coherent, Sentence,' comes into play.

# The power of the Succinct Coherent Sentence

When considering a problem statement, it is vitally important that it makes sense grammatically and is as concise as possible; long, convoluted, all embracing, multi-hyphened, bullet pointed, waffling, repetitive, circuitous, multi-paragraphed, or judgemental statements (get the idea), although relatively easy to construct, allow for sloppy thinking and do not cut to the chase.

## Shift to a higher plane

Keeping the sentence short and leaving out superfluous words is critical to clearly defining the problem. A short problem definition takes your thinking to a higher plane forcing you to focus on the core issue. This happens in practise when carefully listening to someone describe their situation. Often after a lot of talking, they may reach the point at which, while jabbing a finger at their knee, they say, 'You know what really gets me; it's being told that I am lazy.' There it is again, the 'As it is' plus the negative feeling, which together equal the problem.

The aim is to help people (and yourself) reach this moment of great clarity, which concisely describes the problem. Once you have done this you will know that you have defined the problem because you will feel that it really does fit. By this I mean that when you say the statement it feels right and seems to come from inside you, from your gut, not as if it is coming from out to one side of you as if you do not own the statement. The other test of fit is knowing that, when you express it to another person, you will not waiver if challenged. Instead, when visualising the scene, you see yourself looking the person in the eye and saying "That is exactly how it is," confident that the statement is not judging, labelling, assuming, or generalising.

*A young woman described how, over a long period of time, her manager had made many unflattering comments about her report writing and how, in recent times, he had started to criticise her in front of others. The behaviour, although low-level, was ongoing and very corrosive to the woman's confidence and she found the whole thing extremely upsetting, especially being criticised in front of her peers. However, the thought of confronting her manager triggered all sorts of filters about what would happen: chief among them being that it would most certainly ruin her career prospects. She decided to leave. Fortunately, she learnt to clarify the problem, which up until then, she had buried under the usual steaming pile of self-judgements, assumptions, and generalisations. With a bit of listening from a colleague, she clearly described the various aspects of the behaviour that she was unhappy about and the effect they were having on her that collectively equalled the problem. After rehearsing what she was going to say, she asked for a meeting with the manager where she confronted him. "When you criticise my writing, especially in front of others, I feel demeaned." Full stop! No backfilling, no justification, just that sentence.*

The manager's reaction was to apologise profusely, and claim that he did not realise the effect that his behaviour had been having. The woman followed up by telling him that she needed the behaviour to stop, immediately. And it did. No repercussions, no third world war scenarios: quite the opposite. From then on the manager treated her with a newfound respect and the relationship improved markedly.

Many people have recounted similar stories in which seemingly insuperable problems, handled appropriately, resulted in positive outcomes. The real challenge lies in overcoming the strident self-talk of "Yeah! Right! We all know what really happens."

If the woman had angrily confronted the manager with a whole lot of assumptions, labels and other filter-generated stuff, the powerful essence of her story would have been lost. The discussion could easily have degenerated into a slanging match along the lines of what she had originally feared. Most of all, the woman was very surprised with how easily things had changed and, bearing in mind that she was confronting a problem, it had actually improved the relationship: the opposite outcome to that usually predicted by our filters.

*As it is + negative emotion (filters) =*
*Experience (problem)*

## Owning the problem

You **always** own the problem; you cannot hang it on someone else. Inevitably, at some point, you will lose sight of this simple fact but the problem is always yours: yours to play with, yours to reflect upon, and consider. Happily, you cannot own someone else's problem, which is why the "We have a problem . . ." approach does not work. You have the problem; you can invite others to join you in resolving it, but it is still yours. Others have their own problems to deal with, some of which may be a version of your problem but their problems are never the same as yours.

## The office argument

What if you, as manager, came across two of your staff having a loud and acrimonious dispute in the main office? It is likely that you would want to find out what was going on so as to fix their dispute. The trouble is that by doing so, you are now fixing their problem to resolve your problem, and your problem is not their problem. By focusing on resolving the others' problem you have, in effect, limited your options.

Your problem could be 'I am deeply concerned about the impact that your behaviour is having on the rest of the team.' Confronting the pair with such a statement frees you to apply any number of solutions (one of which may involve resolving their dispute) but you are not locked into that one option. The simple act of retaining ownership of your problem enables you to keep on pressing for a resolution. The difference with regard to your sense of control can be dramatic.

## Quick test

Without pondering over it, answer yes or no to the following question:

Have you, at some time in your life, at home or work, experienced a problem with one or more of the following—planning, training, trust or communication?

If you answered "Yes" to any of the topics, look again; each one is a solution. **Planning** may be the solution to services not being delivered on time. **Training** may be the solution to customers receiving poor service. More **trust** may enable people to rely on the word of others. Better **communication** may lead to the number of errors going down, perhaps the area of the actual problem.

These examples serve to demonstrate how easily we are seduced into accepting solutions that are masquerading as problems. I have seen whole teams of very experienced people beaver away over long periods of time on what they mistook to be a problem when it was actually a single (possible) solution to whatever the problem was: I say possible because, if you have not clarified the problem, how can you know that your proposed solution is going to fix it?

# The problem with solutions

Why does it matter if you focus on a solution thinking that it is the problem? Because the moment you focus on one solution, you automatically discount all the other possible solutions. You have fallen into the trap that I mentioned when covering the problem-solving journey and it is highly likely that, instead of finding the optimal solution, your efforts will spawn yet more problems.

*The problems that you are wrestling with today may be the outcome of solutions put in place yesterday*

## A weekend in London

*One Christmas, the managing director of a London-based software development company phoned me and asked if I could get over there within the next couple of days to work with his executive group. He described how the company was in serious financial strife and his executive team, comprising eight very experienced managers, was engaged in ongoing intra-sectional warfare with serious arguments and accusations flying around regarding whose fault it was. The situation was at the top end of serious.*

*After travelling for thirty hours, I arrived at Heathrow Airport on a Thursday afternoon and had a dinner meeting with the Managing Director (MD) to get his view on things. Next morning the MD, his managers and I gathered in a large meeting room set to spend the next three days talking about what was going on and how we could fix it. The atmosphere was very tense.*

*I started by asking each manager to give their own view on the situation. Well, that livened things up, as each manager blamed the other. (Engineering) "If it wasn't for sales selling products that weren't ready, this wouldn't have happened." (Sales) "If engineering had got the product ready on time and it didn't have bugs in it, it certainly would have been okay." (HR) "We constantly get urgent requests for staff needed 'yesterday' when they know full well that it's impossible to get staff that easily" . . . and so on.*

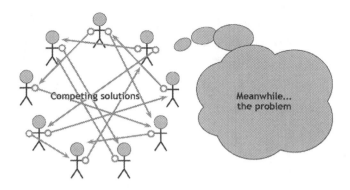

*The conflict was so deep that, just to get them into the right frame of mind and become familiar with the problem-solving process, I had to get the group to work on a less contentious matter that I had spotted. Incidentally, without calling it problem solving, I outlined a process for the workshop so that we could develop an agenda for the order of business. The essence of it was to agree on the problem, agree on where they wanted to be (preferred situation), spend time understanding the problem, list a whole heap of possible solutions and, finally, develop an action plan: all the stuff we covered in earlier chapters.*

*To cut to the chase, it took us one and a half days (can you believe it?) to all agree on a short coherent problem statement, namely "We are concerned that the company is going to fold within the next few months."\* That was it! Once* *out in the open, the problem was rather obvious but, unfortunately, it had become buried under a great steaming heap of horse manure, mainly made up of the usual assortment of favourite solutions, assumptions, judgements, labels and generalisations: little chance of spotting, let alone agreeing on, the problem.*

*\*Note that this was the group's problem statement. The statements of the individual managers were more along the lines of "I am worried that I will not be able to pay the mortgage." (I have softened the expressed feelings here.)*

## The group's journey

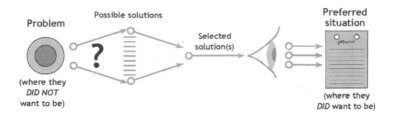

*The moment the group agreed on the problem, the atmosphere changed dramatically to one in which they had let go of their favourite solutions and were ready to focus on resolving things. The change was palpable and we comfortably moved on to exploring and understanding all the little*

'As it is' contributions (the causes) that had given rise to the problem before succinctly describing their preferred situation. We then listed a range (a long list) of possible solutions salted, of course, with each member's favourite solution (any one of which, after due consideration, could have ended up being a part of the subsequent Action Plan).

By this time a combination of jet-lag and the effort of facilitating the process had left me feeling quite tired so, once the group had listed possible solutions for it to evaluate, I gave them one day to prepare a presentation of their action and time-bound plan: their solution for getting to their preferred situation. And off I went back to the hotel to sleep for the rest of the day.

Sunday morning, I arrived at the venue wondering what I would find. To my delight, the group had carefully evaluated the range of possible solutions which included ideas such as close the company, merge with a key competitor, stop selling for several months, raise more capital, lay people off, and freeze the development status. At the conclusion of the evaluation process they developed a very good presentation of their chosen solution and its associated action plan. The atmosphere was great and things were humming along. Moral of *the story: you cannot solve a problem if you don't know what the problem is.*

*Until there is agreement on the problem, individuals or groups flail around debating various possible solutions none of which can be tested to see if they fit the problem.*

## Sources of conflict

There it was, a real life drama created as a result of everyone focusing on their favourite solution and then presenting it as a problem, which brings me to the point that, contrary to intuition (stand by for incoming dogma),

*It is competing solutions, not problems, that generate conflict*

Solutions giving rise to more problems—it just doesn't sound right.

## Trench warfare

Trench warfare, sometimes euphemistically referred to as positional bargaining, is where each party—the protagonists—adopts a position (solution), and then defends it to the death. The supporters of each side provide fresh munitions, in the form of encouragement, such as "How unfair! I would never put up with that," or "You go for it" and similar helpful comments. Basically with trench warfare your options are: get bigger, better, or more, munitions or dig a deeper trench and keep your head below the parapet (assuming that you have had the foresight to fit a parapet). Then hang in there.

## Trench warfare

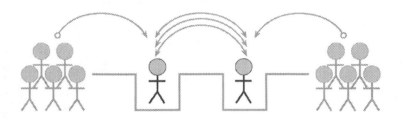

## Going for a compromise

This process ensures that both parties go away feeling equally hard done by. Consider the common or garden, management-union pay dispute, conducted in much the same manner as a Japanese Noh play (sadly, without the music) where everyone knows the format and outcome. This positional bargaining play goes something like this:

Management: "We cannot afford a pay increase."

Union: "We demand 10 percent."

Protracted arguing during which both parties retreat to consult their executive teams.

Resumption of headbutting where both parties agree to a split-the-difference compromise of 5 percent with the pain evenly spread and both parties equally unhappy.

The sad part is that each party's fixation on its favoured solution precludes other, more creative, solutions.

## The surprise solution

Remember the bit in the problem-solving journey about not jumping in at the 'Your good idea' stage? Surprisingly, solutions can create a major blockage to progress. Presenting someone with a solution to something, when they were not aware there was a problem, is a bit like poking them in the eye with a sharp stick. It comes as a surprise.

On the part of the recipient, the instinctive reaction to the surprise solution is to reject the idea with "We haven't budgeted for that" or similar; which is not surprising when you consider that they have been caught on the hop and not had the opportunity to travel the journey with you.

## Shifting the goalposts

A better way to approach things is to shift the goalposts, cross out the solutions and shift the focus onto understanding and agreeing on the problem. This could be done via a question such as, "If we did do X what would change?" This way you draw others into travelling with you on the problem-solving journey so that, when you arrive at the point of considering possible solutions, it is in the light of mutual understanding.

### Shifting the goalposts

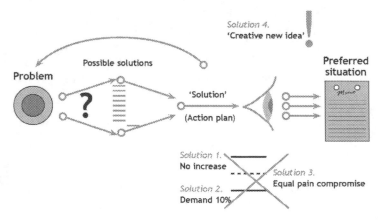

## Stress and solutions

There is always a long list of possible solutions and slugging it out over one or two effectively puts blinkers on your creativity. The very nature of a problem means that there is always some level of stress associated with it (otherwise it would not be a problem) and one of the side effects of this is that, as the stress increases, the list of available options seems to decrease. This effect is particularly evident when the stress is very high at which point you will often hear people say, "If you really understood (my world of filters) you would realise that there is only one option." Mind you, politicians use the same line to try to convince us that their idea is the only idea, the 'We had no choice' syndrome.

*As your stress level increases, the number of perceived options decreases*

## Lifelines

Curiously, the problem is usually one of the things that the conflicting parties can agree upon. It is one of the lifelines, and by that I mean a point that can be agreed upon even when a particular solution can't be found. The idea of lifelines comes from what happens when a tug prepares to take a large vessel in tow. Rather than fire over a heavy steel hawser—impossible to rocket over to the other vessel and likely do a lot of damage on the way—the recue-crew fire over a very light line (seagoing terminology for a rope). They then attach the light line to a heavier line and the crew on the ship being rescued haul it across. Finally, using the heavier line, they haul a steel towing-hawser into place. Similarly with problem solving; rather than going directly to a solution, first find points on which you can agree then you will be well placed to discuss possible solutions.

In addition to agreeing on the problem, other lifelines include agreeing on the preferred situation, agreeing on a combined list of possible solutions, agreeing on a set of guiding principles to align behaviour and agreeing on the problem-solving process. The combined effect is that, as the parties travel along the journey together, they create an atmosphere in which there are enough points of agreement for them to start exploring the solution.

## Who owns the problem?

This chapter has been quite a journey, and I will close by reminding you that clarifying the problem is of prime benefit to you because **the problem is always yours** and, as a fully functioning adult, this is as it should be.

Then you have total control over it—not over 'As it is' but over your experience of 'As it is.'

*It is not what happens that matters, it is how you respond to what happens*

## Helping yourself and others to regain control

When working with others, whether on an organisational or personal basis, it can be tempting to solve their problems for them. Frankly, at that moment, a "Have you tried X?" is often quicker and easier, not to mention that being a 'super solver of problems' can feel rather good. However, the quick fix comes at a price because what you are doing is effectively de-skilling those around and creating dependency on you as they beat a path to your door. "This isn't working." "Oh, better go and ask Mary, she'll know what to do."

There is little future in having others keep coming to you for the answer because, as the source of knowledge, you become trapped in your present situation; no time to do other perhaps more challenging things and too important in your current role to be moved to another role because you are now the lynchpin. Far better to evolve the skills of others so that they sort out their own problems and are not constantly beating a path to your door for pat answers in what is the result of a self-fulfilling cycle set up by you.

## The art of crafting better questions

When travelling the problem-solving journey, there are questions that help people to work their own way through the process, and questions that encourage the travellers to address aspects of what it is that they are experiencing; all while being treated as fully functioning adults.

With the journey in mind, here are some questions that help you to break out of self-inflicted, self-fulfilling cycles by guiding others to reach their own resolution rather than constantly looking to you for the answer. I have included a number referring to the point being addressed in the problem-solving journey. Many stages overlap, so be careful to apply your judgement and common sense when considering the connections.

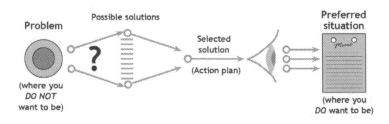

## Better questions

a) See it 'As it is' **(3)**
   Recall events: "Tell me what happened." "What has been going on?"

b) Capture the essence (**1**)
   Paraphrase, summarise: "What's the nub of what happened?" "In a nutshell, what's been going on?"

c) Look around **(3 and a bit of 2)**
   Consider similar situations: "Have you seen this happen in other projects?" "Ring any bells?"

d) Examine 'As it is' **(3)**
   Consider causes and where other wants to be: "What do you think led to this happening?" "How did this come about?" "Where do you want to be?" "How do you want it to look?"

e) Explore options **(4)**
   Look at ways to improve the situation: "How could you improve the way it's being done?" "What are your options?"

f)  Extend learning **(2)**
    Consider new perspectives or applications:
    "How could you apply this learning to other
    projects?"

g)  Evaluate usefulness **(2)**
    Put the matter/this conversation, into context:
    "What did you gain from this?" "How useful
    has this been?" "Has this helped deal with the
    problem?"

**Adopt better and bigger questions**

While considering the matter of asking questions, you
might bear in mind that what you get back depends
on what you ask, so it pays to consider "What would
be an even better question here?" And, having thought
up the answer to that, move on to ask yourself "What
would be a bigger question?"

**Examples of better and bigger questions**

1.  Rather than asking your team leader "How is the
    project going?' a better question may be "Which
    aspects of the project implementation need
    improving?" A bigger question could be "How
    could we improve the implementation of all our
    projects?"

2. Rather than asking a customer "How are sales of Wonder Widgets going?" it may be better to ask, "What can we do to help you improve the sale of Wonder Widgets?" However, a bigger question could be "How could we promote the sale of Wonder Widgets through your international outlets?"

The outcome of asking better questions can be quite dramatic but the opportunity is lost if you do not bother to pause and carefully consider your questions beforehand.

# So, what happened?

At the start of the book, we left the story of the two managers with them seated at either end of the couch in my office, each facing away from the other and avoiding eye contact; the situation looked hopeless with little chance of a breakthrough.

Once I got over a momentary sense of "What can I say? What can I advise? What can I offer?" I simply paid attention to the process (the 'how we do things' as distinct from 'what we are working on') and started by asking each of them, separately, to outline the situation as they saw it. They stated very clearly that each did not trust the other and, furthermore, neither could stand the other. One said that things were so bad that she had already resolved to go to the employment court while the other said that he was planning to lodge a personal grievance claim against the company.

Their stated positions were so firm that there seemed little room to influence things. After each spoke, I thanked them for saying what needed to be said.

If anything, the situation was worse than I had first thought and again, for a brief moment, the thought "I have no idea how to fix this one" flicked through my mind until I reminded myself that I did not need to fix it. These people were fully functioning adults who, although welcoming some assistance, were still responsible for what they did next. Again all I needed to do was pay attention to the process: listen, help clarify the problem, develop an understanding of what was happening, look to the future, and decide on an action plan.

There seemed little point in spending too much time discussing the future as each party was adamant about following their respective plan: file a personal grievance/go to the employment court. Instead, I drew a picture of the Self-fulfilling Cycle and, with reference to that, explained how I saw things, with their beliefs influencing their actions and thereby the next moment. I also pointed out the stark truth that their intended plans would generate a 'next moment' comprising even more distress and that it would not be an easy path. Drawing the 'trench warfare in action' diagram, I also talked about how their small company had split into two groups, each supporting one of the parties in the conflict and encouraging them to 'go for it.'

At this point, things went a little quiet and in the pause the woman quietly observed, "You know, it seems to me that we have a choice of either sorting this out or digging the trenches deeper." I was quite startled by the comment and had not seen it coming. It was a huge turning point in the proceedings. I let the comment hang in the air, before saying that there was not much more we could do that day (we had been talking for around an hour). I suggested that they go away, think about what we had discussed and, if they thought it would be helpful, I would be open to participating in a further session: their call. And away they went in their separate cars back to their company a short drive away.

Half an hour later the phone rang. It was their company director. "What did you do?" His question caused a momentary flutter of the heartbeat as I wondered what had gone wrong. "Nothing special," I said. "When they left me they seemed to be fine." "Well," he said, "I cannot believe it. They are talking to each other for the first time in months. I am dumbfounded!" He asked again, "What did you do?" I related what had happened: that at the conclusion I had had no expectation of a positive outcome and that I had left it to them to think things over in the light of their reflections and my observations.

And that was the last time the managers and I met. They worked out an amicable plan for how they would work together and things settled down. I also suspect that they saved themselves a lot of anger, bitterness, disappointment, and money.

The point of the story is that there was no way that I could have come up with their plan; one that they would truly own. Although they were displaying behaviour that was not that of a fully functioning adult, they still deserved to be treated like one.

# Closing thoughts

As you deal with the inevitable outcomes of the human condition, the journey that you are on is your own. You are the resident expert on how you live your life and no one else has such an abiding interest in your wellbeing. I say this because so often I come across people attempting to create dependency on whatever it is that they are proffering inasmuch as they continue to assume that they hold the key to your progress.

Always be careful to retain control of your journey and avoid handing your power to others either by behaving as a victim or by buying in to actions that result in dependency. However, having said that, expert information or advice, where appropriate, is great because you can take it or leave it. A bit like going to the doctor, it pays to give due weight to the opinion of someone who has spent many years studying the subject but, ultimately, you are responsible for the health and well-being decisions relating to you. I regard my doctor as my (highly experienced) research assistant and we get on just fine.

The example of how I work with my doctor captures the need to balance the courage to be independent with the necessity of being interdependent, sometimes for your very survival: a 'yin *and yang' intertwining of the two. Too often the emphasis goes on being independent at the* expense of others.

## On your journey—

- Acknowledge the problem. There is a temptation to not see a problem for what it is, to try and look on the bright side, as often happens in the advice people give to someone who is stressed. I think that it is better to consider the worst that is likely to happen. Then, having contemplated it, and realised that you can deal with it, to let it go (even if only with one hand at first . . . ☺).

- Always look to where you want to be—focus on it and firmly grasp it (with your spare hand . . .).

- Remember that there is **always** more than one solution to whatever is happening (actually there are many).

- When considering possible solutions, be careful that you are not just looking at variations on the same option. It is very easy to slide into this. For example, you may decide that the answer to your problem is to sell your business and then proceed to think up different ways to achieve a sale. However, your preferred outcome may be to exit the business, to which there are many options, among them leasing it or giving it away.

- Before proceeding with your chosen action plan, be sure to check it against the many facets of the problem to see how well your solution fits. Best to avoid having to parachute cats in!

On your journey the tools covered are just that, tools. If you were a builder and I came along with a bunch of fancy new tools, we could explore what the tools looked like, what they were designed for and what they were capable of but it would be rather presumptive for me to say, "Now go and build a such and such." In response to that sort of request, I would expect you to (politely) explain that you are a qualified builder and, subject to the local requirements, will build whatever appeals to you. Likewise with this book, I am not advocating that you do anything in particular with the information because only you can judge what is appropriate.

With the above in mind, I do hope that you use what we have explored to create meaningful and sustained shifts in how you lead yourself and others. Even though it is often advocated that we have to live life in the fast lane, my personal aim is to be more productive (in whatever way you wish to define that) with less effort, less stress, more fun, and more fulfilment.

My very best wishes to you.

Ian

# Index

## V

## W

# Notes

Frankl Viktor, Man's Search For Meaning, Simon & Schuster, 1984

Haidt Jonathan, The Happiness Hypothesis, Basic Books, 2006

# About the author

Ian Oldham has been facilitating leadership development programmes for over twenty five years. His work incorporates insights into problem solving, facilitation, conflict resolution, organisation efficiency, process improvement, strategic planning and team building and has been delivered in Australia, China, Russia, UK, USA, and New Zealand.

Working with senior executives from leading organisations around the world, Ian's programmes are transformational and universal and have benefitted people in research, hospitality, IT, telecommunications, broadcasting, medical practice, project management, real estate, software development, unions, government, science, employer groups and not-for-profit organisations.

Ian has a range of qualifications (electronics, commercial flying, quality assurance, industrial engineering), executive experience in aviation, manufacturing and retail and owned and operated several companies including an outdoor adventure company.

## Practical and principled approach

Extensive practical experience led to Ian's transformational, dross free, down to earth approach which delivers immediate and sustained benefits. At his workshops, Ian focuses on what really matters and makes it safe for participants to experiment as they explore their transformational leader role, learn to handle change, manage difficult situations with ease and deal with unhelpful behaviour. His passion for continuously evolving concepts, processes and tools strongly encourages participants as they shift their viewpoints, transform their operating style, and apply their learning to what really matters—their business and personal lives.

## Workshop feedback—

". . . truly inspirational and an amazing facilitator"

"I recommend the programme to anyone looking for improved performance"

". . . met my expectations and more"

"Returned to work and home life uplifted, thoughtful"

## Contact Ian Oldham

ian@shiftinggears.co.nz        www.shiftinggears.co.nz